A Nature Lover's Guide to Seeing God

*Reflections and photographs
by a biologist and a pilgrim*

BOB & EVELYN MCDONALD

BGP

Blue Gum Publishing
Website: www.bluegumpublishing.com
Email: enquiries@bluegumpublishing.com
Newcastle, NSW, Australia

Unless stated otherwise, all Bible verses are from the New International Version.
Scripture quotations are taken from The Holy Bible, New International Version® NIV® Copyright © 1973 1978 1984 2011 by Biblica, Inc. TM. Used with permission. All rights reserved worldwide.
Scripture taken from The Message. Copyright © 1993, 1994, 1995, 1996, 2000, 2001, 2002. Used with permission of NavPress Publishing Group.

Cataloguing in Publication Data:
Title: A Nature Lover's Guide to Seeing God
ISBN: 978-0-6450446-2-1
Subjects: Nature; Creation; Christianity; Photography

Design and layout by initiateagency.com
Edited by Capstone Editing
Front cover photograph: Spa Pool, Hamersley Gorge, Karijini National Park, Western Australia.
Rear cover photograph: Rock platform at sunset, Putty Beach, New South Wales.
Acknowledgements photograph: Aerial view of James Price Point, Kimberley Region, Western Australia.
Foreword photograph: Dales Gorge, Karijini National Park, Western Australia.
Introduction photograph: Knox Gorge, Karijini National Park, Western Australia.
All land-based photographs (with the exception of those in Reflections 10, 19 and 27) were taken with a Fujifilm X-T1, X-T2 or X-T4 camera using a range of Fujinon XF lenses. Aerial (drone) photographs were taken with a DJI Mavic 2 Pro.

A Nature Lover's Guide to Seeing God

Reflections and photographs by a biologist and a pilgrim

BOB & EVELYN MCDONALD

Black-winged stilt (Himantopus himantopus)

Acknowledgements

We would like to acknowledge the Traditional Custodians of the lands we walk through, photograph and enjoy, and pay our respects to Aboriginal and Torres Strait Islander Elders past, present and emerging. We are extremely grateful for the way they have cared for their lands for over 60,000 years, such that today we enjoy a country with incredible natural and cultural diversity and beauty.

We would also like to acknowledge the work that has been done over a number of generations in setting aside and managing, with limited resources, our system of national parks and conservation areas, and other areas of special natural and cultural significance.

We would especially like to thank Professor John Attia who first suggested the idea of our developing this book and who has given ongoing support and feedback. We would also like to express our appreciation to Sally Smith (Christian editor and writer) and Reverend Graham Wintle for their valuable feedback on the first draft and their encouragement.

We would also like to acknowledge the use of one photo (Reflection 10) that was taken by our son, Peter McDonald. All other photos were taken by us as we had the privilege of exploring our beautiful natural world in Australia, New Zealand, Indonesia and Samoa.

Contents

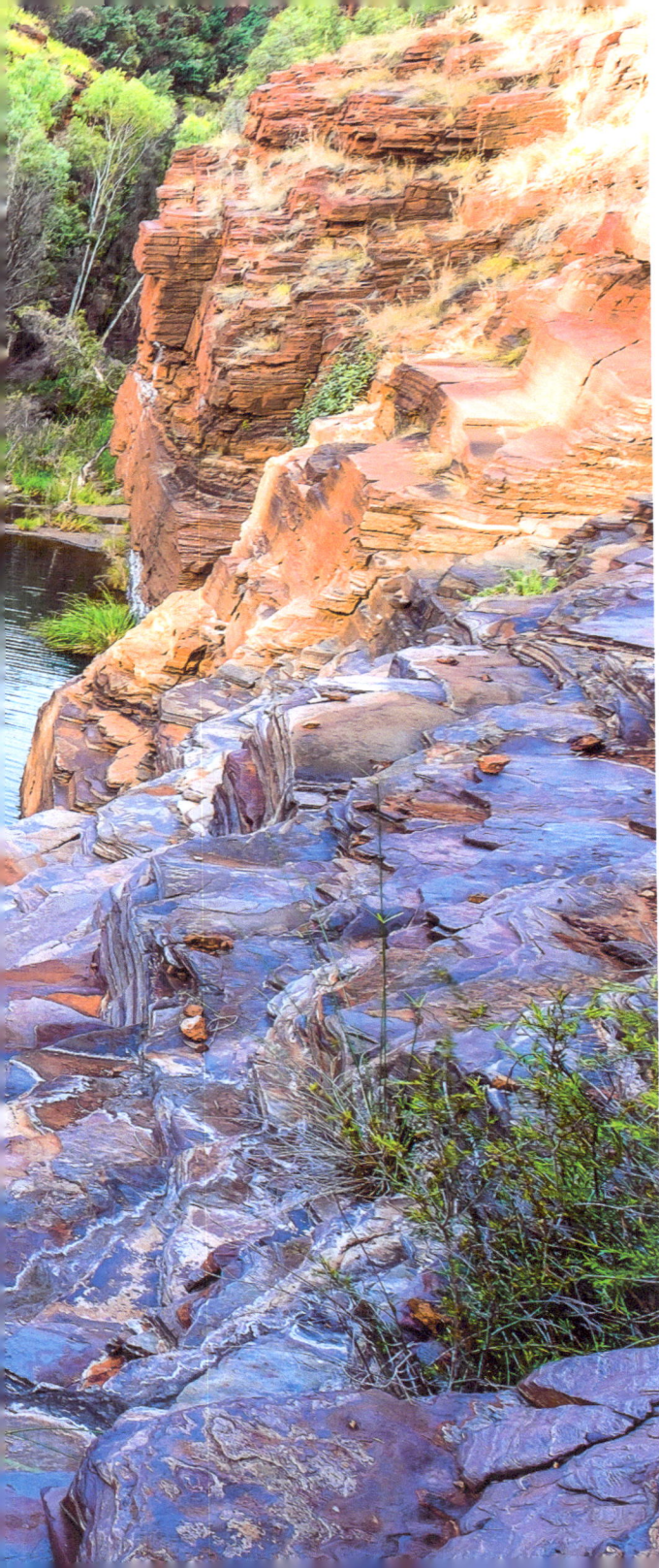

Foreword by Tim Costello AO

In the opening pages of Genesis, we are told that humans were created in God's image and given a divine mandate to care for creation. Creation care is a fundamental building block of Christian faith, so it is incumbent on all Christians to take seriously God's mandate. Our world is changing daily, and we are living in a narrowing window of opportunity - we only have to look to the natural disasters of recent times to see this - fires raging in the Amazon rainforest, powerful hurricanes battering the Caribbean, unseasonal rain in parts of Africa, and drought, flash floods and bushfires in Australia

At the same time, we as Christians are called to unveil a pragmatic and inspiring view of a better world. And I believe that as we experience the beauty of God's creation, hearts are changed, and when hearts are changed there is hope for a bright future.

For those of us in the humanitarian sector, the reality of a changing climate has a human face to it. It is a child in a barren landscape with no food to eat, or huddled in a flimsy shelter during a violent storm. As our hearts soften towards God's original plan for His earth and our eyes are open to the world around us, we are able to embrace the need to love and protect our environment, and therefore fulfil the greatest commandment to love God and love others.

Through this book, Bob and Evelyn have given every reader a chance to experience the majesty of God's creation from the comfort of their home. Not only this but the scientific facts included throughout the book allow each reader to learn new concepts and ideas, stimulating the mind and imagination.

I truly believe that all Bible-reading Christians should be 'greenies', because creation carries the imprint of the Maker. As Christians, we strive daily to know our Maker more, and learning more about His creation through this book provides us with an opportunity to grow closer to Him. Allow the amazing photography to wash over you as you experience His creation in new ways each day.

I want to encourage Christians as they read this book to be transformed by the beauty of God's creation and delve deep into the related Bible studies, but then go on and take a step further by looking at the reality of our world today and asking ourselves and the Holy Spirit "What can we do to maintain and enhance God's world as He truly intended it to be?" Then we can go from here being transformed by Him and into the world to make a difference.

Introduction

So many of us are drawn to nature. We delight in it, relax in it, are awed and amazed, rejuvenated and inspired by it. Increasingly, research shows that time spent in nature is, indeed, mentally and physically therapeutic. Even simply looking at photographs of nature can have positive effects on people.

This book, through its photographs and words, celebrates something of the beauty, diversity, detail, creativity, design, form and colour that is present in nature or, as it is so often named—Mother Nature. This extraordinary earth, unlike any other planet in the solar system, holds an incredible array of life, from the tiniest microorganisms to the mammoth creatures of the land and sea, which is continually being sustained and renewed. The order, complexity, mathematical precision and interconnectedness of living things within ecosystems, in addition to the sheer beauty of nature, lead us to think that this is neither a random nor a coincidental phenomenon, nor one without purpose.

Choosing to run with the idea that nature is not a series of coincidences without purpose leads to the recognition that it has intentionally been designed, formed and ordered. Therefore, being in nature takes on a further dimension. We are led to understand that the one behind it all is a thoughtful designer, a master of complexity, a skilful artist, a lover of diversity, a life-giver and one who sustains.

On its opening page, the Bible states *'in the beginning God created … And God said, "Let there be …" and God made …' (Genesis 1)*. Later, it declares that *'since the creation of the world, God's invisible qualities—his eternal power and divine nature—have been clearly seen, being understood from what has been made' (Romans 1:20)*. The Bible unequivocally begins with God creating—bringing into existence the seas and land, the sun, moon and stars, vegetation and creatures. This created world, discerned by its Creator to be *'very good'* (Genesis 1:31) is God's 'first book' to all humankind; considering or contemplating creation can lead us to understand something of what its Creator is like.

The Creator's further attributes, plans and purposes, particularly concerning humanity, are revealed through 'the second book'—the Bible. Its story has been recorded by a diverse range of people: from a reluctant leader who began life as a carefully abandoned baby to a renowned king of the people of Israel; from a citizen of Persia to forthright and, often, ridiculed prophets; from an impulsive fisherman to a scholarly tent maker; from a doctor to a former tax collector in Roman-controlled Judea. Yet, despite the diversity of its writers, a consistent story unfolds of the Creator and His plans and purposes for both humankind and the creation in which we have been placed as likewise created beings (Psalm 104), who have been given a unique role as people made in the image of God (Genesis 2:15).

In the following pages, we draw on both the 'first book' and the 'second book' to reflect—in image and word—on our Creator God and His intentions for His creation and us as part of it. Each photograph captures a different aspect of creation. For each of these, we provide background and, where appropriate, include basic scientific details in recognition of the significance of science in helping us to understand what is happening in the world around us and in leading us to see (even more) how incredible is our Creator God. In reflecting on the images, we draw from various parts of the Bible to consider not only what has been written about creation but also what has been written about its Creator and humanity. We share all of these with you, in the hope that you will see more of God and be drawn closer to Him, that your appreciation of the amazing nature of His creation will grow and that He will lead you in your response to all this.

To God be the glory.

Our Story

Bob

My lifelong interest in and love for our natural environment began while growing up on a beautiful rural property near Tamworth in north-western New South Wales. Some of my earliest memories are of spending many hours alone exploring the river and timbered areas that were part of the farm. This was encouraged by my parents, who were also happy to wait long hours on car trips while I ran, walked and explored the surrounding national parks.

View from Mueller Hut, Mt Cook/Aoraki National Park, New Zealand.

My interest in nature led me to major in Geology and Philosophy and, later, Biology at the University of Newcastle. Around this time, through involvement with a local group also interested in bushwalking and nature, Evelyn and I were asked to co-edit *Hunter Natural History*, a quarterly magazine about local flora and fauna, including enjoying it and ensuring its future.

During this time, I had no religious affiliation but was intensely involved in a search for truth, meaning and purpose. For this reason, I majored in Philosophy. As part of this searching, I began studying Eastern religion with the help of an Indian guru (teacher), who was sent from overseas to Sydney and who regularly came to teach a group that we set up in Newcastle. As I undertook this study and practised meditation and yoga over several years, I began to perceive that 'God' and nature were indistinguishable; that God was in all and was all—in other words, a pantheistic view of the world.

Several years later, this changed dramatically when, following 10 years of searching, God led me to see that what I was searching for centred on Jesus Christ. Overnight, my love for nature gained a totally new perspective—everything I saw in the natural world around me reflected God's incredible handiwork and sustaining power! I could not help but be drawn in worship, through looking at the stars in the night sky, high mountains covered in snow, green forests, ever-changing seas or amazing plants and animals. Nature is still my favourite place in which to walk, climb, swim, snorkel, enjoy the company of others, worship and pray.

After my surrender to God, there followed two years at Sydney Missionary and Bible College and then pastoral and overseas ministry. Upon returning to Australia and unsure of what to do, I completed a PhD in Biology and spent time seeking to share the wonder of nature through teaching and research at the university. During this period, my eyes were opened further to the incredible handiwork of God, whether by seeing His creation at the micro-level through an electron microscope or exploring processes and chemical pathways at sub-cellular and cellular, organ or whole organism levels. All this reinforced my belief that, in no way, could it be the result of chance—rather, that it reflects purposeful creation by an incredible God.

I continue to explore and seek to photograph various aspects of God's creativity and power and enjoy sharing these with others, whether through photography or bushwalking. I am very thankful that God has graciously drawn me into a relationship with Him and that He continues to reveal new things about Himself and His amazing world.

Evelyn

I grew up in my grandmother's house, which was directly opposite one of Newcastle's lovely beaches. My bedroom was regularly bathed in the light of the morning sun as it rose over the ocean. As I moved from childhood to teenage years, I became increasingly aware of the moods and changing colours of the ocean and sky in different weather and seasons. Due to our location, we not only enjoyed the beauty and peace of a tranquil ocean and sky but were also exposed to the wilder elements of the weather, such as raging southerly winds, torrential rain and the thunder of waves crashing onto the shore and eroding the beaches. I can remember quite vividly when, one dark night, our front door was blown in by the power of gale-force winds during a wild storm. However, these turbulent storms were not the norm. On weekends and holidays, my friends and I regularly enjoyed exploring the pools in the local rock platform with their small scale and varied marine life—much of which has sadly disappeared—climbing the cliffs rising from the local beach and, of course, swimming in the ever-changing sea.

At that stage of my life, I regularly and happily went to church, joined in Sunday School classes and read my Scripture Union notes on Bible passages, but I had no conscious understanding of God's love, nor did I connect the aspects of nature that I so enjoyed with Him.

Meeting my future husband, Bob, whose main hobbies were bushwalking and nature photography, opened the world further. Many hours were spent walking in and exploring our diverse natural environment. We regularly visited the mudflats on Kooragang Island to observe the migratory waders that arrived in their thousands each year from the northern hemisphere. These amazing birds, with their different characters, shapes, sizes and patterned feathers, were and are still fascinating to observe and sketch. Around this time, I stopped going to church because I felt hypocritical being there—I did not believe the words about God that I was singing or hearing. Instead, I tagged along on my husband-to-be's search for truth.

A few years later, during a teaching placement in a small town west of Newcastle, we had the

Endangered far eastern curlews, the largest migratory shorebird in the world, spending summer on local mudflats.

opportunity to explore the sandstone country around Wollombi. It was there that we discovered, among other things, Australian native orchids—delicate treasures of colour and design almost hidden in the more rugged bush. At the same time, and despite these discoveries in nature, I was sensing what I can only describe as 'something missing' in my life and a longing to go to church. This we did, and the words of the service—about God, forgiveness and Jesus' death—made so much sense. From there began the journey to learning more of God and His ways that continues to this present day, and which I trust will continue until my time on this earth has ended. Throughout the years, our innate love of nature led us to spend school holidays camping in and exploring national parks with our boys. Both of our sons, now adults and fathers, enjoy being 'in nature' very much and sharing it with their children and others. One leads a regular walking group and is an enthusiastic homegrown food gardener, and the other is passionate about ecology, which has been the focus of his studies, work and research.

The incredible colour, detail, design, diversity and beauty of the natural world has long fascinated me. Over time, I have come to increasingly recognise it as evidence of a good, creative and wonderful God, whose love for the world is fully expressed in the life and actions of Jesus, through whom and for whom the world was made and by whom it is held together. Therein lie mystery and majesty and a journey into wonder at the miracle of it all.

Reflection 1:

Heavenly Glory

Background

The Karijini National Park is a 'dark sky' area in the Pilbara region of Western Australia. It is recognised as such because there is minimal light pollution from any human activity. Consequently, on a clear night, the sky is an overwhelming expanse of stars, planets and galaxies, including the incredible Milky Way.

For at least 60,000 thousand years, Indigenous Australians, known to be Australia's first astronomers,[1] have sat under this same Milky Way. They have read not only the lights but also the dark patches. The dark patches in this photo reveal an emu. Its head and the upper part of its body are to the right of the large tree. In Wiradjuri culture, this emu, called Gugurmin, depending on its position in the night sky, can signal the time to hunt for emu eggs. Reading the night sky, Indigenous Australians also gained valuable information about water sources, travel paths and optimum travel times throughout the year.[2] This ancient knowledge is still relevant today, but the increasing degree of light pollution in our world hides what can be seen and read in the beautiful and informative night skies.

On several nights during our stay at Karijini National Park, we made our way to the viewing platform at Joffre Gorge to gaze at the star-filled sky and photograph it against the silhouette of the gorge walls. Out there in the black stillness, it was impossible not to be awed by the spectacular display above and overwhelmed with an awareness of just how minuscule we were under the seemingly never-ending expanse of stars twinkling in the black velvet sky. It was so easy to think of ourselves as insignificant. Yet, in the dark stillness of the night, under those far-away lights and in complete contradiction of that thought, the words of Psalm 8 came to mind.

Reflection

Lord, our Lord, how majestic is your name in all the earth!

You have set your glory in the heavens…

…When I consider your heavens, the work of your fingers, the moon and the stars, which you have set in place, what is humankind that you are mindful of them, human beings that you care for them?

You have made them a little lower than the angels and crowned them with glory and honour. You made them rulers over the works of your hands; you put everything under their feet: all flocks and herds, and the animals of the wild, the birds in the sky, and the fish in the sea, all that swim the paths of the seas.

(Psalm 8:1–8)

We are not insignificant. God thinks of us and cares for us. From the beginning of God's story, He has shown humankind how precious and important we are to Him. This Psalm is simply another expression of this. Although we do occupy a very small space, the author of this Psalm does not even question our significance. He is assured that, in God's eyes, we do matter—each one of us—and that God is very mindful of us. God remembers us. God cares for us.

Like many parents, we have family who lives abroad. We do not see them regularly, but they are very much in our thoughts and prayers. Although they are a long way away from us, 'out of sight' is not 'out of mind' for us. Likewise, according to the Bible, God, who created the earth and life and who might seem distant from us, is, in fact, very attentive and caring towards us. We are neither 'out of His sight', nor are we 'out of His mind'.

Further, the Psalm author continues to say that not only does God think of us and have regard for our needs, but He also has made us co-rulers with Himself. This is extraordinary! The words of verses 5–8 tell us that we have a special place and responsibility in the scheme of things. These verses very much recall Genesis 1:26–28, where our purpose on earth is declared. God made us so that, as His representatives, we might rule. However, post-Fall and throughout history, this word 'rule' has been interpreted through the lenses of cultural bias and human selfishness and, consequently, has been taken to mean 'domination'—selfish control and destructive rule. It has even been used as an excuse for abuse. John Mark Comer put it succinctly in his book, *Garden City*, when he wrote that, as humans, we have a great capacity to either rule in a way that brings life or in a way that is exploitive and destructive and actually diminishes life.[3] In other words, human choice, our choices as appointed co-rulers with God, determine the reality in which we live. They either reflect God's good rule or do otherwise.

We have a special place in God's heart and mind. He has entrusted us with much. This is both a wonderful and an awesome responsibility!

Prayer

Heavenly Father, as the incredible Creator of the universe, of which the magnificent night sky we see is just a small part, it is awesome that you are mindful of us. You care for us, and you desire us to be people who bring heaven to earth. Father God, help us to live as your image-bearers and bring your life and your loving wise care to all that has been entrusted to our care. Amen.

Reflection 2:

Protecting Life

Background

One joy experienced throughout the year is seeing and hearing birds. Australia has 828 species of native birds.[4] Many are strikingly beautiful, engage in intriguing displays and produce melodic calls. Not all our birds, though, are brightly coloured or visually striking. Some are little—even tiny— and mostly brown, such as the thornbills, the gerygones and the scrubwrens. They busily go about their little lives, feeding, nest-building, breeding and raising young. All birds, regardless of size, colour or shape, are an integral part of our diverse ecosystems. One of the delights of birdwatching is to see these creatures go about life in such a seemingly unselfconscious manner, with their food and nesting material provided for.

One such example is the elegantly designed eastern spinebill (*Acanthorhynchus tenuirostris*), which can be found in heath, forests and woodland, east of the Great Dividing Range. You may have seen one visiting flowering shrubs or trees in your house yard. This small (15 centimetres) bird has a fine, curved beak that enables it to extract nectar from flowers, such as the pink grevillea in this photo. Eastern spinebills can also hover like hummingbirds when extracting this sweet food. In the breeding season (August–January), they build cup-shaped nests from twigs, grass and bark, and use spiderwebs to bind these together. At least 18 per cent of Australian birds make use of the readily available webs of Australia's numerous spider species. As spiderweb is adhesive, elastic and strong, the birds use it to 'glue' their nests together; this also enables the nest to expand as the baby birds grow and require more space.[5]

Reflection

Some years ago, when undertaking studies at a Bible College in Sydney, we were asked to write an essay on the topic 'What Deuteronomy teaches about care for the environment'. It was an eye-opening exercise because this book, believed to have been written a few thousand years ago, contains a surprising number of statements relating to the environment and its care. One of these is Deuteronomy 22:6-7:

> *If you come across a bird's nest beside the road, either in a tree or on the ground, and the mother is sitting on the young or on the eggs, do not take the mother with the young. You may take the young, but be sure to let the mother go, so that it may go well with you and you may have a long life.*

The book of Deuteronomy recounts the words of Moses to the Israelites before they entered their new homeland. There, they were to establish a radically different community life. Of Deuteronomy's 34 chapters, many present laws given by God for the wellbeing of both the people and the land in which they would live. These laws are very practical and may surprise any of us who thinks that conservation is a relatively recent concept.

The above verse is one of these. It focuses on a seemingly small aspect of life and is quite specific, but it conveys a crucial principle—that of respecting and protecting life and, in so doing, conserving life and food sources. Those settling into a new land, like people suffering hunger or poverty in many parts of the world today, needed a food supply—God knew this very well. However, in such circumstances, a person was most likely to take everything—the mother and the young or eggs. In the short term, there would be food to eat; however, eventually, a species would be wiped out and, therefore, a source of food for future generations.

An example of this is what happened to the lovely passenger pigeon *(Ectopistes migratorius)* in the New World of America in the 1800s. John Muir, the immigrant Scotsman who became a renowned naturalist in America, recorded what happened to these birds. Within the short space of 50–60 years, the passenger pigeons, estimated to have numbered approximately four billion and whose annual migration darkened the skies, were systematically exterminated. One of the methods was to use sticks to knock the young from their nests, together with the parents who nurtured them.[6] By 1914, the passenger pigeon was extinct.

The purpose of this law in Deuteronomy was to rein in the human tendency to indiscriminately take or wantonly destroy as much as possible without regard for the consequences. The mother bird is to be left free to continue to live and reproduce. Respect for these creatures would, in turn, enhance the Israelites' own life in their new land. God, as the Creator, is the original conservationist. He is concerned for the continuity of the creation He has brought into being. If we define ourselves as God's people and His co-rulers, we, too, should reflect His ways—looking after what has been placed in our care. As God's people, it is our responsibility to promote life and enable it to flourish: *'the earth is the Lord's, and everything in it.' (Psalm 24:1)*.

Prayer

Father God, you know us very well. You know our tendency to want and take more than we need no matter what it is. Father, forgive us. Show us what it means to live wisely and respectfully, in ways that care for your creation and ultimately ourselves. Amen.

Reflection 3:

The Wonder of Trees

Background

Australia has wonderful biodiversity; however, it is under serious threat. Land-clearing, in particular, poses a great risk because trees are a major component of this biodiversity.[7] Trees are extraordinarily beneficial; they stabilise valuable topsoil, absorb carbon dioxide, provide oxygen, produce mulch and nutrients for the soil and give shelter, roosts, food and water to birds, insects, microorganisms and people.

This photo, taken at Mt Cabre Bald in the Barrington Tops National Park, contains *Xanthorrhoea glauca* in the foreground—commonly known as 'grass trees', which are endemic to Australia. Some grow to one metre, whereas others (such as these) can grow to six metres; however, their growth is extremely slow at approximately 0.8–6 centimetres per year. They are one of the many Australian plants that respond to fire with abundant flowering.

For Indigenous Australians grass trees provided food, drink, fibre and materials for making tools, such as fire sticks. The thin, spiky leaves also produce a valuable waterproof resin that was traded for other items.[8] To the first European settlers, these plants were unlike any others they had known. As one of the earliest flowering plants, they are a living fossil.[9] Actually, although tree-like, they are neither a grass nor a tree.

Generally, trees are associated with the colour green. In terms of psychology, green is linked to life and restfulness. In terms of physiology, our eyes have three types of photoreceptor cells—called 'cones'. These cones contain photo-pigments and are designed to sense wavelengths. Together, the cones work to communicate the colours we see to the brain. In daylight, our eyes most easily pick up the wavelengths of green light, which means less strain on our eye muscles.[10] How amazing is this when we consider all the greens in a tree-filled environment and how restful and restorative it is to be in such places!

Reflection

Now the Lord God had planted a garden in the east, in Eden; and there he put the man he had formed. The Lord God made all kinds of trees grow out of the ground—trees that were pleasing to the eye and good for food.
(Genesis 2:8–9)

In this early Biblical text that describes the creation of man (and later, woman), trees are mentioned four times. This is no accident. Trees were fundamental to humans' ongoing existence in a garden created by God and in which He placed them. Trees provided food. However, what is striking about these verses is that the trees are first described as '*pleasing to the eye*' and, following this, '*good for food*'. The man and woman were primarily intended to enjoy being in this God-given green space that was alive with plant life. In this delightful setting, their food was provided. John Mark Comer commented that, in Hebrew writing, the order is crucial;[11] the fact that '*pleasing to the eye*' (the beautiful) precedes '*good for food*' (the practical) indicates that the Creator God wants us to enjoy and appreciate beauty first and foremost and, in particular, the beauty of trees, the sight of which is so restful to our eyes, minds and bodies.

The book of Deuteronomy also gives interesting instruction related to trees. In Deuteronomy 20:19–20, we read the following:

When you lay siege to a city for a long time, fighting against it to capture it, do not destroy its trees by putting an axe to them, because you can eat their fruit. Do not cut them down. Are the trees people, that you should besiege them? However, you may cut down trees that you know are not fruit trees and use them to build siege works until the city at war with you falls.

In claiming the land promised to them, Israel would have to go to war with any nation that did not want to make peace with them. However, in fighting against people, the wanton destruction of trees was forbidden. Trees that provided food were, unequivocally, to be preserved. Indeed, trees not only provide food for people but are also part of dynamic ecosystems that provide pollen for insects, nectar for birds and habitats for insects upon which other creatures feed. The excessive destruction of trees in the event of warfare was to be restrained. In other words, short-term gain was not permitted to override the long-term benefits of preserving trees and, thereby, safeguarding land and conserving food supplies for the immediate and longer-term future.

In making this specific stipulation, God recognises the human capacity to thoughtlessly destroy the environment without regard for the long-term consequences and, particularly in war, often to spare nothing. However, He, the Creator, does have regard for the greater and long-term picture. When God told the Israelites not to cut down the trees that were a source of sustenance, He understood their strategic significance in the ecological context. This importance has not diminished—if only this advice had been heeded in the centuries since, how different might parts of our world be today!

Prayer

Father God, thank you for the trees in our environment. Thank you for both their beauty and their crucial role in life on earth. Father, we mourn actions that have needlessly destroyed them and continue to do so. Help us to recognise trees as essential 'gifts' from you, not simply for ourselves and future generations, but for our environment and all creatures living in it and to wisely act on this recognition. Amen.

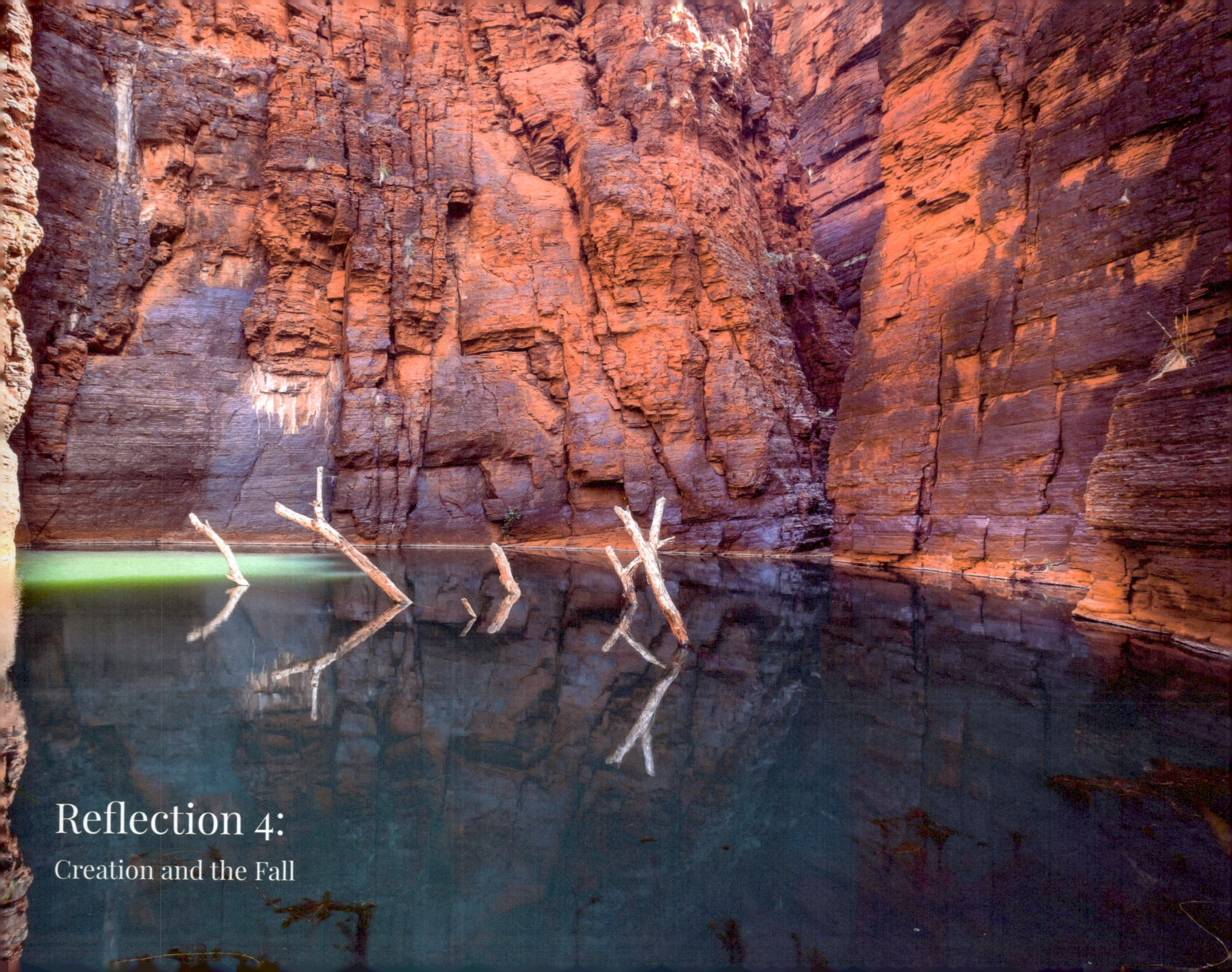

Reflection 4:

Creation and the Fall

Background

Junction Pool is at the end of Hancock Gorge in the Karijini National Park, Western Australia. In this photo, the end of the gorge can be seen to the right, behind the dead tree trunks in the water. This is a Class 6 restricted area that is not open to the public generally, but which can be legally accessed with a local adventure company.

This pool is a striking place. It is here that four, deep red, iron-rich gorges meet—hence the name Junction Pool—and its quiet stillness reflects a beauty that is seen by relatively few.

At the same time, and despite the unique beauty, the signs of death in this place are also very apparent. Further back, in Hancock Gorge (one of the four gorges), is a plaque commemorating the passing of a State Emergency Service volunteer who was swept to his death while trying to rescue two injured people caught there in a sudden heavy storm.

Additionally, the weathered and bare trunks of once-thriving trees, steadily starved of oxygen by constant submersion, now stand starkly like gallows and portend the danger of snags and other logs that possibly lurk beneath the still surface of this secluded and beautiful pool. The towering red cliffs may also conjure up different images for different people. Their imposing presence may be a reminder that these are treacherous places for the unwary or overconfident visitor, whose wrong step might be fatal.

In a very real sense, the beauty of Junction Pool in its stunning setting is marred by the present reality of death and decay.

Reflection

The death and decay of this world, although prevalent and pervasive, are not where the Bible story begins or ends. As beginnings and endings reveal much about the scope and meaning of a story, it is significant that the Bible history begins not with death and decay or even people, but with God. It begins with God creating a vast, beautiful world out of nothing (Genesis 1), and it ends with a beautiful, new creation lit by the glory of God (Revelation 21–22).[12]

After creating man and woman, we read '*God saw all that he had made, and it was very good.*' (Genesis 1:31). However, after the 'Fall'—the rebellion of Adam and Eve—and their resultant expulsion from the Garden of Eden (Genesis 3), it could be reasonable to ask, 'What happened to the rest of creation at this time? Was it still '*very good*'?

Genesis 3 makes it clear that Adam and Eve's rebellion against their Creator has had dramatic consequences. Their sin resulted not only in a disruption to their relationship with God (v23f) and with each other (v16) but also their relationship with the land: '*cursed is the ground because of you*' (v17). This theme is continued through the Old Testament, where we learn that the earth itself, and all its life, is portrayed as suffering or mourning as a direct consequence of sin and rebellion. For example, '*how long will the land lie parched and the grass in every field be withered? Because those who live in it are wicked, the animals and birds have perished. Moreover, the people are saying, "He will not see what happens to us"'* (Jeremiah 12:4).

Hundreds of years later, the Apostle Paul expanded on the consequences of Adam and Eve's sin, stating that all of creation has been subject to futility and enslavement to decay or ruin:

For the creation was subjected to frustration, not by its own choice, but by the will of the one who subjected it, in hope that the creation itself will be liberated from its bondage to decay and brought into the freedom and glory of the children of God. We know that the whole creation has been groaning as in the pains of childbirth right up to the present time. (Romans 8:20–22)

Humanity's fall into sin, as described in Genesis 3, marred creation, which has ever since been in a state of 'frustration'. This joint sense of incompleteness and frustration highlights the interrelatedness of humanity and human choices and the rest of creation.

However, this is not the end of the story. There is hope! Creation, while currently locked into the decay that has pervaded this world since the Fall, exists in the sure hope that it will be set free to participate in the glory to be enjoyed by God's people in the new heaven and earth. It has been noted by many scholars that the idea of creation '*being set free*' strongly suggests that the ultimate destiny of creation—as it is for those who believe in and follow Christ—is not annihilation but a beautiful, fully healing transformation.[13]

Prayer

Lord, we acknowledge that we are guilty of living our lives selfishly—not listening to you nor caring for your creation as we should. We also acknowledge that our sin can have far-reaching consequences for the world around us—consequences that we see and those that we don't see. Help us, we pray, to live our lives truly as new creations in Christ—loving you wholly and our neighbours as ourselves, using our freedom as your children to act justly, wisely and with humility towards all the creation among which we are placed. Amen.

Reflection 5:

Creation's Witness

Background

This scene was photographed in Mt Cook/ Aoraki National Park, New Zealand. After walking to the end of the Red Tarns Track, I (Bob) traversed a steep scree slope above the Red Tarns for spectacular views of the strongly glaciated landscape, including Mt Cook/Aoraki itself. Some features commonly associated with glaciers are seen in the photo—the tarns (small lakes) in the foreground, a lateral moraine (rocks and other debris left on the side of the glacier after the glacier wastes away) in the midsection, two valleys carved out by glaciers (Hooker and Mueller Glaciers coming down from the right-hand and left-hand sides, respectively) and deeply dissected mountains, eroded by the movement of ice and rocks over thousands of years.

A glacier is a thick mass of ice that has formed from the compaction and recrystallisation of snow. Compaction of the ice mass over long periods slowly forces out air bubbles between ice crystals. When this happens, the ice becomes very dense and absorbs a small amount of red light, leaving a bluish tint in the reflected light.

In several countries, including New Zealand, many glaciers have either disappeared or been markedly reduced in size due to human-induced warming climates. Glaciers store approximately 70 per cent of the world's freshwater. If they were all to melt, in addition to other land ice, the sea level would rise by approximately 70 metres, putting millions of people and their livelihoods at risk.[14]

Even though this photo shows only an extremely small part of God's creative handiwork, it bears witness to and declares His glory, whether this be the processes of glaciation that continuously carve and shape the landscape, the alpine grasses in the foreground, the tarns and the small aquatic life that live in them, the low-lying moisture-laden clouds or the majestic mountains!

Reflection

While humanity's fall into sin marred creation such that, ever since, it has been in a state of 'frustration', it is stated that creation is continuously sustained by Christ through whom and for whom all things were made (Hebrews 1:3; Colossians 1:16). Creation does not belong to us, and neither does it exist for us. It exists for God and, as such, is a witness to His glory. Several verses highlight this, in addition to God's care for and delight in it. Many of these are found in the Psalms. The following is just a small sample. Firstly, we read that creation sings out the glory of God loudly and clearly:

The heavens declare the glory of God; the skies proclaim the work of his hands. (Psalm 19:1)

Not only do the heavens continuously (from the Hebrew—ongoing, never ceasing) testify to God's greatness, but Psalm 104 provides a vivid picture of the natural world and the Creator's dynamic, caring role, which brings enjoyment:

He makes springs pour water into the ravines; it flows between the mountains. They give water to all the beasts of the field; the wild donkeys quench their thirst. The birds of the sky nest by the waters; they sing among the branches. He waters the mountains from his upper chambers; the land is satisfied by the fruit of his work. (Psalm 104:10–13)

Further on, we read that the earth abounds with his creatures, all of whom are dependent on Him for life and all that is good:

How many are your works, Lord! In wisdom you made them all; the earth is full of your creatures … All creatures look to you to give them their food at the proper time. When you give it to them, they gather it up; when you open your hand, they are satisfied with good things. When you hide your face, they are terrified; when you take away their breath, they die and return to the dust. When you send your Spirit, they are created, and you renew the face of the ground. May the glory of the Lord endure forever; may the Lord rejoice in his works. (Psalm 104:24, 27–31)

Throughout the Psalm, the picture is of a Creator God who is extravagant with His creativity, who delights in beauty and in satisfying the needs of His creation. As has been noted by one Biblical scholar, 'the God of the Bible is not the god of the Deists who makes a world and then leaves it to its own devices; this is a God who remains at work in the world He loves, and which bears witness to His glory'.[15]

Well-known former Christian writer and pastor Eugene Peterson strongly encourages us to experience, with all our senses, God's wonderful creation in all its fulness:[16]

'The lived quality of Genesis chapter 1 fuels my efforts in trying to raise the blinds in the living quarters of so many people I know and have known; to raise the blinds and get them out of the house between Sundays to enter into this vast, rhythmic extravaganza, seeing and hearing, tasting and touching and smelling what God has created and is creating by his Word: sky and earth, plants and trees, stars and planets, fish and birds, Jersey cows and basset hounds, and the crowning touch, man and woman—look at them! … 'And God said … and it was so … and it was good'.' Good indeed!

Meditation

For his invisible attributes, namely, his eternal power and divine nature, have been clearly perceived, ever since the creation of the world, in the things that have been made. (Romans 1:20)

Reflection 6:

Searching for God

Background

On the second day into the three-day Routeburn Track walk in South West New Zealand, we decided to depart temporarily from the main track to search out a good vantage point for photography. We climbed a sidetrack to Paddy's Point, from which we had beautiful views over the Routeburn Flats and valley and from where this photo was taken. The following day, we descended through the beech rainforest along the right-hand side of the valley and crossed the fresh snow-fed river several times before completing the walk.

The New Zealand Department of Conservation describes this world-renowned walk as 'the ultimate alpine adventure, taking you through ice-carved valleys and below the majestic peaks of the Southern Alps/Kā Tiritiri o te Moana'.[17] The track is well marked and maintained, with several huts to stay in along the way. Tracks like this provide people with great opportunities to spend some healthy time away from city life and enjoy God's majestic creation.

The twisting river valley in the photo is not only a beautiful example of God's creative handiwork but was also one of the main routes used by Māori people on their journeys to the west coast in their search for pounamu (greenstone). Pounamu are a group of hard green stones found on the South Island of New Zealand. They continue to be highly valued by the Māori, and hardstone carvings made from pounamu play a key role in Māori culture. Geologically, the rocks are usually nephrite jade, bowenite or serpentinite.[18] With the arrival of Europeans, some of the early explorers among them also ventured up this valley in search of pastoral land and gold, but their search for the latter was mostly unfruitful.

Reflection

Over the centuries, people have sought things of value. Immigrants and refugees are usually seeking a new life for themselves and their families. In medical research, many teams are searching for vaccines against dangerous viruses. Some people are searching for inspiration, while others are searching for happiness and purpose in life.

The Bible reveals that people have been created to live in relationship with our Creator God—deep inside, there is often a longing to do just that. As St Augustine confessed, 'Thou hast made us for thyself, O Lord, and our heart is restless until it finds its rest in thee'.[19] As such, we are encouraged to earnestly seek God with the promise that when we do, we shall find him: '*you will seek me and find me, when you seek me with all your heart*' (Jeremiah 29:13).

In response to this, some may ask—can we seek and find God in nature? Romans 1:20 informs us that '*since the creation of the world God's invisible qualities—his eternal power and divine nature—have been clearly seen, being understood from what has been made.*' Through nature, we can certainly learn how wonderful, how powerful, and how 'beyond us' (divine) God is. However, this knowledge, which is often ignored, will not lead us into fully knowing God and how much He loves us. John's gospel records Jesus saying to one of his disciples, '*I am the way and the truth and the life. No one comes to the Father except through me. If you really know me, you will know my Father as well*' (John 14:6–7). In the book Romans, Paul wrote that being in a right relationship with the Creator depends not on a knowledge of God's existence (e.g., through nature), but rather on surrender to the risen Jesus Christ who underwent death by crucifixion for our sins and was raised from death to life: '*if you confess with your mouth that Jesus is Lord and believe in your heart that God raised him from the dead, you will be saved*' (Romans 10:9). In the search for a relationship with God, the gateway is Jesus.

Not only do people search for God, sometimes at a subconscious level, but God also searches us and our hearts: '*search me, God, and know my heart; test me and know my anxious thoughts*' (Psalm 139:23); '*he who searches our hearts knows the mind of the Spirit, because the Spirit intercedes for God's people in accordance with the will of God*' (Romans 8:27).

These statements are both a reminder and an encouragement for us. They remind us that nothing is hidden from God, and they encourage because we are precious to Him and He can reveal to us where a change in our thoughts or actions—in our very being—is needed. He also sees where prayer for us is needed. So, rather than being like Adam and Eve, who tried to hide from God in their nakedness and embarrassment (Genesis 3:10), we can work with Him and let His searching of us be fruitful, a means of transformation for good, knowing that He is with us and for us.

Prayer

Search me, O God, and know my heart today; try me, O Saviour, know my thoughts, I pray;
See if there be some wicked way in me; cleanse me from every sin and set me free.
Lord, take my life, and make it wholly Thine; fill my poor heart with Thy great love divine;
Take all my will, my passion, self and pride I now surrender; Lord, in me abide.[20]

Reflection 7:

What's in a Name?

Background

This small ground orchid was photographed in a section of open eucalypt forest in the Raymond Terrace area of the Hunter Valley, New South Wales. It was growing naturally in a clump with several others. If you were the first person to discover it, what name would you give it?

Based on its remarkable shape, with an obvious duck-like bill and head, it is referred to as the flying duck orchid (*Caleana major*). Can you see the other parts that look like a duck flying? This small orchid grows up to 50 centimetres tall, and each flower is approximately 2 centimetres long. It is found in eastern and southern Australia and is often difficult to see unless being explicitly searched for.

Why was it designed in this way? Most likely, this occurred to attract insects such as male sawflies, one of its natural pollinators. The insect is attracted to the orchid by pheromones (chemicals) that mimic the sex pheromones of receptive female sawflies. When the sawfly touches the extremely sensitive labellum (the part at the top right that resembles the head of a duck on the U-shaped 'neck'), it snaps shut and immediately traps the insect temporarily in the sticky body of the column at the base. The insect deposits any pollen it may be carrying and picks up more before being released to fly to the next orchid for the process to be repeated. Insects such as sawflies make good pollinators because they fly and can, therefore, pollinate many plants in a short time.[21]

How incredible is God to design such a specific mechanism and scent for the reproduction and the sustainability of this amazing little 'flying duck'!

Reflection

While the name of this intricately made orchid reflects its appearance, the names of God in the Bible do not give us any insight into what He looks like. His appearance is mostly a mystery. However, the names of God do give us insight into what He is like:

> And now the cry of the Israelites has reached me, and I have seen the way the Egyptians are oppressing them. So now, go. I am sending you to Pharaoh to bring my people the Israelites out of Egypt.' … Moses said to God, 'Suppose I go to the Israelites and say to them, "The God of your fathers has sent me to you" and they ask me, "What is his name?" Then what shall I tell them?' God said to Moses, 'I AM WHO I AM. This is what you are to say to the Israelites: "I AM has sent me to you". (Exodus 3:9–14)

In this last statement, we are given one name that God uses for Himself—*ehyeh*—'I AM', from the Hebrew verb *hyh*, 'to be'. In using this name, God tells Moses and the Israelites that He really does exist—but not just 'exist'. Alec Motyer, the renowned Old Testament scholar, wrote that this Hebrew verb means more than simply 'exist'. It means 'to be actively present'.[22] Further, His actions are for our good. In the same book, Exodus, we read how God, in releasing the Israelites from slavery in Egypt, took them on the most creative and unexpected route—through the middle of a sea! We also read that, day and night, He continued to be actively present, eventually leading them to the new homeland He had promised.

In John's gospel in the New Testament, Jesus is recorded as specifically making seven radical 'I AM' statements: '*I AM the bread of life*' (John 6:35, 41, 48, 51); '*I AM the light of the world*' (John 8:12; 9:5); '*I AM the gate for the sheep*' (Jn 10: 7, 9,); '*I AM the good shepherd*' (John 10:11, 14); '*I AM the resurrection and the life*' (John 11:25); '*I AM the way and the truth and the life*' (John 14:6); and '*I AM the true vine*' (John 15:1). His use of '*I AM*' clearly echoes its use by God. In doing this, Jesus unequivocally declares that he is God. Although this claim infuriated the Jewish religious leaders, to people hungering for God, these statements clearly spoke of what He was like. In Jesus, an actual historical person, God was physically and actively present among the people of the region, eating and sleeping, walking and talking, teaching and guiding, healing and restoring, rebuking and comforting and ultimately giving his life for the world that He loves.

Following his resurrection from death and return to the presence of God, Jesus sent the Holy Spirit—the Spirit of truth—to be actively present with his disciples. The Spirit of the living God empowered them to be people who could not help but speak and tell of what they had seen and heard. Through their words and actions, God was present, growing a community of believers, His church.

Prayer

Father, Son and Holy Spirit, your appearance is a mystery; but thank you that you reveal so much of what you are like in your names. Thank you for your active presence throughout history, releasing, saving, leading, guiding and strengthening. Thank you that you honour us, your children, with your indwelling, Holy Spirit—your living and active presence. Help us to honour you by heeding your Spirit to bring your glory into whatever situation we are. Amen.

Reflection 8:

The Greatness of God

Background

On a summer evening, when a storm was in progress over Newcastle, we captured the scene in this photo. The sheer immensity of the 'light show'—both the cloud-to-ground flashes and the intra-cloud or cloud-to-air flashes (sheet lightning)—was stunning. While the human-made city lights beamed out beneath, as evidence of human presence, invention and enterprise, there was a very real sense in which the lightning spectacular in the air was so much more powerful and vast and yet, at the same time, and in this instance, incredibly contained. There was no destruction. It was amazing!

All of us have witnessed the power of lightning, which results from an electrical discharge caused by imbalances of positively charged protons and negatively charged electrons between storm clouds and the ground, or within the clouds themselves. As a child growing up on a farm that seemed to attract more than its share of lightning, I remember often lying in bed feeling quite scared as lightning struck the large eucalypt trees just near our house, resulting in a terrifying explosion. The following morning, I would venture out to see the effect of that transient lightning strike. The sap and water beneath the bark had instantly heated, expanded and exploded, causing the tree to split.

Although lightning bolts may seem to be quite large, their average width is just two to three centimetres; however, they can be up to five times hotter than the surface of the sun![23] To calculate how many kilometres away a thunderstorm is, we can count the number of seconds between the lightning flash and the thunderclap and then divide that by three. However, it is possible for lightning to move well ahead of a storm and hit the ground without any obvious warnings—hence the term 'a bolt from the blue'.[24]

Reflection

Phenomena such as a dramatic storm can speak to both the absolute might and greatness of the Creator God and our limitations as humans. This is the exact point made in Chapters 38–41 of the book of Job. This four-chapter poem contains the Creator God's words to the man Job. Job has suffered much and is desolate. It is into his utter desolation that God speaks. In so doing, He gives Job an extraordinarily intimate insight into who He is. By talking to him directly, God not only shows Job that He has not abandoned him but also, through the questions He asks of him, leads him to see that His wisdom and power are beyond human comprehension:

> What is the way to the place where the lightning is dispersed, or the place where the east winds are scattered over the earth? Who cuts a channel for the torrents of rain, and a path for the thunder to water a land where no one lives, an uninhabited desert, to satisfy a desolate wasteland and make it sprout with grass? Does the rain have a father? Who fathers the drops of dew? From whose womb comes the ice? … Do you know the laws of the heavens? Can you set up God's dominion over the earth? Can you raise your voice to the clouds and cover yourself with a flood of water? Do you send the lightning bolts on their way? Do they report to you, 'Here we are'? (Job 38:24–29;33–35)

Through the ages, human research and discovery have brought us much knowledge and invention. Scientists can explain how many natural phenomena work and, to some extent, the functions they serve. However, questions remain about how and why they all began, and how and why all that has been brought into being is sustained. God tells Job that He is the Creator and Sustainer of both the elements and creatures.

It is easy to forget that we are but creatures—created alongside the plants and animals and given life by God. Accepting our creatureliness is perhaps not easy because it means accepting our limitations. Job was led to see this, and King Solomon also understood it. He expressed it in Proverbs 3:5–6: 'trust God from the bottom of your heart; don't try to figure out everything on your own. Listen for God's voice in everything you do, everywhere you go; He's the one who will keep you on track. Don't assume that you know it all' (The Message).

It is easy to slide into a self-sufficient mindset and to take pride in our knowledge and power. Yet, there come times when circumstances throw us off balance; our 'control' over our lives is lost, and they seem 'out-of-control' and to not be going the way we envisioned. In such times, we can blame God and be engulfed further by our own limited understanding, or we can do as Solomon advises and 'trust God from the bottom of your [our] heart; don't try to figure out everything on your [our] own' (Proverbs 3:5). God knows the future, and it is in His hands. He understands the big picture and the detail and how both do work and will work together. Moreover, He loves us—He is for us.[25] We are urged to trust Him wholeheartedly because He loves us wholeheartedly.

Prayer

Heavenly Father, so much in the natural world testifies to your greatness and glory. Give us eyes to see afresh your eternal power and divine nature through the natural phenomena around us. May our hearts and minds be truly awed by you. Help us to listen for and heed your voice in our daily life. Amen.

Reflection 9:

Tree of Life

Background

In landscape photography, over the past 10 years, the use of drones to capture aerial views of the patterns, colours, textures and scenes of our incredible earth has increased significantly. This photo was taken on the Kimberley coast at Roebuck Bay, south of Broome, during a period of king tides—with a difference of nine metres between low and high tide. The large tidal variations along this coast have been of immense benefit to the traditional owners for tens of thousands of years. Following some of the highest tides in the world, the exceptionally low tides expose and provide access to vast intertidal reefs, rock shelves and mudflats, offering rich areas for hunting and food gathering.

During king tides, when the saltwater pushes inland for distances varying from one hundred metres to kilometres in length, tree-like dendritic patterns, such as those in the photo, are often formed. The colours of these tree-like features vary in accordance with the colour of the surrounding sand and mudflats and the type of vegetation that grows alongside them. While some of these dendrites may look desolate and lifeless, they are, in fact, often associated with a rich marine life, such as small invertebrates and larger creatures—like the birds that feed on them. Research has shown that these tree-like streams of saltwater are full of food particles. This results in these and the surrounding mudflats having some of the richest biodiversities of any mudflats in the world, with hundreds of species of benthic invertebrates at an average density of 1,287 individuals per square metre.[26] The most common groups of species identified by surveys here are bivalves, worms, snails, tusk shells, crustaceans and echinoderms—all vital elements of an incredible living ecosystem.[27]

Reflection

The tree-like patterns created by the flow of water into rich tidal mudflats recall another tree image:

> *Blessed are those who find wisdom, those who gain understanding, for she is more profitable than silver and yields better returns than gold.*
> *She is more precious than rubies; nothing you can desire can compare with her.*
> *Long life is in her right hand; in her left hand are riches and honour.*
> *Her ways are pleasant ways, and all her paths are peace. She is* **a tree of life** *to those who take hold of her; those who hold her fast will be blessed. By wisdom the Lord laid the earth's foundations, by understanding he set the heavens in place: by his knowledge the watery depths were divided, and the clouds let drop the dew. (Proverbs 3:13–20; emphasis added)*

The book of Proverbs reflects the wisdom of King Solomon, who specifically asked God for '*a discerning heart*' (I Kings 3:9), and whose prayer was answered with the result that: '*he was wiser than anyone else … And his fame spread to all the surrounding nations*' (I Kings 4:29–31). In these verses, he expands the analogy of wisdom as female to include a tree of life. Wisdom is a tree of life, not necessarily to everyone, but '*to those who take hold of her … who hold her fast*'. Choosing to do this and acting on it is essential.

The tree of life is first mentioned in Genesis; it grows in the garden in which Adam and Eve were placed. After eating from the 'other' tree—the tree of knowledge of good and evil—Adam and Eve were barred from eating from the tree of life, which would have caused them to live forever in their fallen and decaying state. However, in Revelation, the last book of the Bible, the tree of life features again—this time, it is in the new city, where it is a source of sustenance and healing to all present in the new heaven and earth (Revelation 22:2).

In between the garden of Genesis and the new heaven and earth of Revelation, these verses in Proverbs 3 also tell us of another tree that gives life—wisdom. A living tree pulses with life within and without. It grows, produces leaves, fruit and seeds, and is a refuge and host for a wide range of life—animals, birds, insects and microorganisms. It stabilises the earth around it, shelters, protects and nourishes. As we seek and apply God's wisdom, are we becoming like this—life-enhancing, safe to be with, nurturing and nourishing for ourselves and others?

In verses 19–20 of Proverbs 3, Solomon moves from the tree of life to the bigger picture—the ultimate source of life-giving wisdom, God. He reflects that it was with wisdom that God created this amazingly complex miracle of a world in which we are placed. With wisdom, He factored in the sustainability of the systems and processes and the coordination and interconnectedness needed to nurture life.

So, King Solomon tells us to seek, hold on to and live by wisdom from God. In the words of the Biblical scholar, David Atkinson, 'all Wisdom's paths are peace, wholeness, health and contentedness—not only in our inner heart but also in our outward network of relationships in the world'.[28]

Prayer

Lord, thank you for the many pictures in your word that help us to understand truths. Just as a tree of life flourishes and blesses other life, may we, too, take hold of your wisdom—that tree of life—and live accordingly, that your will may be done on Earth. Amen.

Reflection 10:

The Creature with a Bad Reputation

Background

The desert death adder (*Acanthophis pyrrhus*), photographed by our son Peter while carrying out research into snakes along the MacDonnell Ranges in Central Australia, frightens most people. This specimen appears particularly large because it has puffed itself up with air in response to the presence of a potential threat—the researcher!

The desert death adder grows up to 65 centimetres long and is a 'sit-and-wait' predator that uses its narrow tail tip to lure small creatures close to its body. It will then strike, bite the prey and wait for it to die before swallowing it. Like all other death adders, it strikes fast and is dangerously venomous; the bite is often fatal if not treated.[29]

Research has given us clear guidelines about what to do if bitten by a snake. The injected venom does not move directly into the bloodstream; rather, it moves very slowly through the lymphatic system. Therefore, immediately immobilising the bitten person and applying a compression bandage significantly slow the movement of the venom, allowing more time for help to arrive. When bushwalking in more remote locations, in addition to an appropriate first aid kit, it is responsible practice to carry a personal locator beacon for such emergencies. However, not every bite from a venomous snake necessarily results in envenomation. Snakes may 'dry bite'—that is, puncture the skin or outer clothing without injecting venom. There are different reasons for this, such as the snake not releasing enough venom or the release of venom not coinciding with the bite.[30]

Perhaps you find it difficult to look at the snake in this photo; you cannot wait to turn the page to something 'more pleasant'. On the other hand, you may be someone who sees the incredible design of these creatures and recognises that they are another fascinating part of our natural world.

Reflection

Serpents or 'snakes' are mentioned in the Bible over 30 times. Although snakes themselves are not evil creatures, they certainly get a mixed rap.

After being led out of Egypt, the Israelites grew impatient and angry with Moses and God for bringing them away from the familiarity of Egypt, albeit oppressive, to wander in the desert (Numbers 21:4–5). Due to their grumbling and rebellion, God sent venomous snakes among them, resulting in many deaths. Some came to Moses, acknowledging their wrong, and asked him to pray to God to take away the snakes. God responded by instructing Moses to '*make a snake and put it up on a pole; anyone who is bitten can look at it and live*' (Numbers 21:8). Moses did this; '*when anyone was bitten by a snake and looked at the bronze snake, they lived*' (Numbers 21:9).

Over 1,200 years later, while speaking with an enquirer named Nicodemus, Jesus referred to this incident as he prophesied the type of death that he would endure—namely, being nailed to and lifted up on a wooden cross: '*just as Moses lifted up the snake in the wilderness, so the Son of Man must be lifted up, that everyone who believes may have eternal life in him*' (John 3:14).

These Old and New Testament verses reveal a problem, the solution and an outcome. In Numbers 21:5, the problem to be addressed was the Israelites' attitude and resulting words of complaint against God and Moses—they were in 'glass-half-empty' mode. In John 3:14, Jesus indicates that he 'must' be lifted up (crucified); the reason for this is the collective sin of humanity in all its manifestations, and primarily that of putting ourselves in place of God. In Numbers 21:8–9, the solution provided by God in response to prayer was to represent the death-inflicting snakes as a bronze artefact on top of a pole, which, when looked up at—an act of obedience in itself—would produce healing. In the case of humankind's collective sin, Jesus as the son of God offered himself to receive the judgement we all deserve through his death, which, under Roman rule, was by crucifixion; he, too, was lifted up, but on a wooden cross. The outcome for those Israelites who looked up at the bronze serpent on a pole was healing. Similarly, those who look to Jesus and accept his gracious and loving act can, through him, enter into a relationship with their Creator that brings healing and hope and life in its fullness.

Not only was Jesus raised up on a cross, but he was also raised to new life to sit at the right hand of the Father. Similarly, '*God [has] raised us up with Christ and seated us with him in the heavenly realms in Christ Jesus, in order that in the coming ages he might show the incomparable riches of his grace, expressed in his kindness to us in Christ Jesus*' (Ephesians 2:6–7).

Prayer

Lord God, this powerful story featuring snakes—so readily demonised in our thinking—also reveals that you provide the means to turn situations around. Our part is to respond.

We pray that your loving means of restoration enacted in the crucifixion and resurrection of your son, Jesus Christ, will continue to be made known throughout the world so that many more may see, respond to and experience a restored relationship with you, the gracious giver of life and breath and everything good. Amen.

Reflection 11:

Beauty in Darkness

Background

Caves are fascinating places because they constitute a 'hidden' world for many of us. While they can be beautiful places to explore, they can also be quite dangerous. Most of us would remember the rescue of 12 boys and their coach from a flooded cave in Thailand in 2018. Interestingly, the two Australian doctors who were centrally involved (Dr Richard Harris and Dr Craig Challen) used their platform as Australians of the Year to encourage young people to get away from screens and to be adventurous and explore our wonderful outdoors!

The photo shows a section of Rainbow Cave, located in the Munmorah State Conservation Area on the Central Coast. This is an example of a littoral sea cave, perhaps one of the most interesting and colourful on the Eastern Australian coast. The cave is large, with fascinating marine life in the dark pools and passageways that extend well back into the cliffs behind. The main entrance is usually underwater, and the cave itself filled with the surging sea. For this reason, it is also referred to as the 'Hidden Cave'.

It is clear from the photograph why it is called Rainbow Cave, but how have the beautiful rainbow colours come into being? They are due to various types of calcifying algae that absorb different wavelengths of low-intensity light. The low-light environment requires specialised strategies to enable the algae to survive. In addition to the algae, in the bottom right of the photo are bright red sea-tulips (*Pyura gibbosa gibbosa*), which are surrounded by extensive dark brown cunjevoi (*Pyura stolonifera*). Cunjevoi, an animal, live in large colonies on rocks around the edge of the low-tide mark; when trodden upon, they often squirt a well-aimed jet of water. 'Cunjevoi' is an Aboriginal name; they were once a common food source for those who lived along the coast.[31]

Reflection

Once it is safely accessed, it takes a while for our eyes to penetrate the darkness of Rainbow Cave to see the surprising and extravagant beauty that lies within. Similarly, the greatest event in the Bible and in history is also a place where darkness and beauty meet. This is vividly summarised by George Bennard's hymn, *The Old Rugged Cross*.[32] Although it was written in 1912, the words of this hymn capture the truth of the darkness and beauty that are inextricably associated with the crucifixion of Jesus:

> Oh, that old rugged Cross so despised by the world, has a wondrous attraction for me
> For the dear Lamb of God, left his Glory above, to bear it to **dark** Calvary
> In the old rugged Cross, stained with blood so divine
> A wondrous **beauty** I see, for the dear Lamb of God left his Glory above to pardon and sanctify me. (emphasis added)

Crucifixion was one of the most painful and shameful ways to die under Roman law and reserved for political rebels, slaves and criminals. According to the Bible, Jesus was none of these, nor had he done anything wrong; yet, he willingly undertook to endure such a death. In this cosmic event that was marked by 'darkness coming over the whole land' (Luke 23:44), Jesus bore the full weight of the sin of the world and, for a time, lost his deep and intimate fellowship with God, his Father. Is it possible for us to fully understand how utterly devastating this was for Jesus?

We must look beyond the darkness to see the beauty of the act. Therein lies the beauty of God's deep love for His creation, which includes us, and the beauty of Jesus' self-giving obedience to his Father's plan. Due to His deep love and grace, God planned and accomplished this rescue act and then brought Jesus back to life. Of his hymn Bennard used to say, 'I really didn't write it. I was merely the instrument God used.'[33]

Another hymn writer, Isaac Watts, (1674–1748) also saw the beauty and darkness of the cross:

> When I survey the wondrous cross on which the Prince of glory died, my richest gain I count but loss and pour contempt on all my pride
> See from his head, his hands, his feet, sorrow and love flow mingled down!
> Did e'er such love and sorrow meet, or thorns compose so rich a crown?[34]

Much like Bennard and Watts, when we reflect on the meaning of the cross and Jesus' death, which was, indeed, brutal and unimaginably physically and spiritually painful ('my soul is overwhelmed with sorrow to the point of death' [Mathew 26:38]), we are drawn in amazement to the deep, self-giving love of God for us. The cross by itself is ugly and cruel, but when we look past the darkness, the willingness of Jesus ('he who was without sin' [2 Corinthians 5:21]) to undergo the punishment required by divine justice for the world's collective sin is a beautiful act that reveals the heart of the Creator God. Not surprisingly, Bennard's favourite verse in the Bible was John 3:16–17: 'for God so loved the world that he gave his one and only Son, that whoever believes in him shall not perish but have eternal life. For God did not send his Son into the world to condemn the world, but to save the world through him.'

Prayer

Jesus, we praise you for your beautiful sacrificial love; your willingness to endure the darkness to bring us light. In our own challenging times, mould us and fashion us so that our lives may reflect the beauty of your love and grace. Amen.

Reflection 12:

The Wisdom of God

Background

This imposing creature is the powerful owl (*Ninox strenua*)—this particular bird was photographed in a small rainforest in a nearby reserve. Throughout the 10 minutes in the late afternoon that we spent photographing it from various angles, this owl never once took its large beady eyes from us.

The powerful owl is the largest of Australia's owls and usually inhabits the moist forests of Eastern Australia. Its main prey is possums, although it often catches flying foxes, gliders, roosting birds and, sometimes, small ground-dwelling animals such as rabbits or marsupials. The powerful owl forages mainly in trees, swooping down upon its prey and taking it with its large, clawed feet. These owls roost by day, perched in dense tree foliage, often with the previous night's prey held in their talons. In this particular location, one bird has occasionally been seen with the remains of a flying fox! The powerful owl can sometimes be heard at night in the bushland around cities, uttering its distinctive and penetrating 'woo-hoo' call. This owl mates for life (in some cases, for over 30 years) and pairs defend their territory throughout the year. The male prepares the nest in a tree hollow (usually a vertical hollow in a large tree that is at least 150 years old), and he provides the female and young with a constant supply of food during the early part of the nesting period.[35]

Tree hollows, which can take 100–200 years to form, are critical habitats not only for the powerful owl but also for much of our Australian wildlife. The fact that 17 per cent of our bird species, 42 per cent of our mammals and 28 per cent of our reptiles rely on hollows in trees for their survival[36,37] is a good reason to preserve trees, be they alive or even appearing to be dead.

Reflection

The Bible refers to the owl over 20 times. It is considered unfit for food: '*but these you may not eat … the little owl, the great owl, the white owl*' (Deuteronomy 14:12,16). It is also associated with isolation and desolation: '*I am like a desert owl, like an owl among the ruins.*' (Psalm 102:6). In the Western world, owls are often associated with wisdom. This may originate in Greek mythology, where the symbol of the owl was associated with the Greek goddess Athena, the goddess of wisdom and patron goddess of Athens. God's wisdom, however, is not associated with a creature but with the most unlikely and unexpected of objects—a cross.

After completing school, I (Bob) went on an intensive 10-year search for answers to questions that pressed me about life and purpose. For this reason, I studied Philosophy for four years as part of a science degree. Why? Because I wanted to find answers from the wise people, the philosophers of the past 2,500 years—Socrates, Plato, Spinoza, Kant, Hegel and many others. What did I learn? First, it was useful to study Philosophy as it helped to provide a lifelong grounding in critically assessing the assumptions and logic behind what is said and written. On the other hand, I found that man's wisdom did not lead me anywhere fruitful in my quest for wisdom and truth; it failed to reveal eternal truths about our world and our purpose in it.

Six years later, God helped me to see that the truth I was looking for began with Jesus Christ and that my life needed to be reoriented around him and his teaching. At that time, a Bible passage jumped out at me that helped to explain, ever so clearly, why my earlier searching had not provided answers to my pressing questions:

Where is the wise person? Where is the teacher of the law? Where is the philosopher of this age? Has not God made foolish the wisdom of the world? For since in the wisdom of God the world through its wisdom did not know him, God was pleased through the foolishness of what was preached to save those who believe. Jews demand signs and Greeks look for wisdom, but we preach Christ crucified: a stumbling block to Jews and foolishness to Gentiles, but to those whom God has called, both Jews and Greeks, Christ the power of God and the wisdom of God. For the foolishness of God is wiser than human wisdom, and the weakness of God is stronger than human strength. (1 Corinthians 1:20–25)

There is something about God's wisdom that is simple yet incredibly profound; it is not something that man would devise. It had to have come from beyond man. True wisdom, wisdom about life and purpose, about this world and its Creator, has one source only—God. Who would have dreamed that God, through His love, would give His Son, through whom the world was made and is sustained, to be shamed and crucified on a wooden cross and, in doing this, pour out love, satisfy justice, provide forgiveness and deal with evil?

Meditation

God called Jesus Christ to what seemed an absolute disaster. And Jesus Christ called his disciples to see him put to death, leading them to the place where their hearts were broken. His life was an absolute failure from many standpoints except God's. But what looked like failure from a human perspective was a triumph from God's because God's purpose is not the same as human purpose.[38]

Reflection 13:

Delighting in Creation

Background

During a bushwalking holiday on New Zealand's South Island, we set out early one morning to climb up to Mueller Hut in Mt Cook/Aoraki National Park. Although physically challenging, this is one of the most stunning walks in this park. The track climbs high above the valley to be surrounded by the peaks where Sir Edmund Hilary developed his love for mountaineering. As we started the walk, Evelyn spontaneously raised her hands in thanksgiving to God for the beauty and peacefulness of the scene before us.

International research has shown that there are significant benefits for all who might spend time in creation.[39,40,41,42,43]

We will become more relaxed. According to research, it only takes five minutes to experience the relaxing effects of nature. Physical activity has also been demonstrated to help people relax; therefore, if being outdoors in nature replaces inactive pursuits with active ones, the benefit is further increased.

When we leave our concrete 'jungles' for a few hours in forests and parks, we will experience increased immune function. Although further research is needed, some scientists postulate that phytoncides, the airborne chemicals that plants emit to protect them from rotting and from insects, play a role in this.

Our risk of heart disease and high blood pressure will be lowered. Although there may be many contributing factors, people who spend more time in nature generally have lower blood pressure, lower cortisol levels and a lower pulse than people who spend more time indoors or in an urban environment.

Studies have shown that spending time outdoors in our natural environment can also improve our creative thinking and our perspective on the challenges we may be facing.

Our vitamin D levels rise. Sunlight on the skin can lead to the creation and activation of vitamin D that may promote vitamin absorption, strengthen bones and help prevent some chronic diseases.

Reflection

To delight in something means to have a '*high degree of pleasure … extreme satisfaction … joy … enjoyment … rapture*' from it.[44,45,46] At some time, most or all of us have delighted in our experience of creation. This may be due to one or more of the aforementioned benefits, or perhaps because we have simply enjoyed the sheer beauty of a natural scene, such as the sight of majestic mountains cloaked in snow and glowing in the early light of the rising sun or the last rays of the setting sun.

In Psalm 37, we are told to '*take delight in the Lord, and he will give you the desires of your heart*' (Psalm 37:4). To delight in God is to enjoy Him and all He is. To take this further, it could be argued that, as His creation is an expression of who He is, to delight in God is also to delight in that which He has brought into being and sustains—to delight, for example, in the 'milk and honey' perfume and the golden form of the wattle blossom is to delight in the one who made it. Or is it?

Many who do delight in nature, who enjoy its beneficial effects, stop there and do not continue to consider where it has come from or who it is for. The Pulitzer Prize-winning author Richard Powers, before writing his novel about trees, *The Overstory*, testified to experiencing a revelation. It came to him that creation, such as ancient forests and all that is in them, are not ours to do with what we like. They do not belong to us.[47] This accords with what God says in the Bible. Creation was brought into being by God and for God, and humankind was placed within it and entrusted with godly rule over the living creatures. As it says in Psalm 24:1–2, '*the earth is the Lord's, and everything in it, the world, and all who live in it*'.

When we do delight in creation and read it as God's 'first book', reflecting His grandeur and glory and power and might, it is not only humbling but also worship for God wells up from within us. However, can we, with all integrity, worship on the one hand and, on the other, live in ways that may promote neglect of or failure to care for creation or, even worse, abuse of it?

Nicky Gumbel, the Anglican Vicar of Holy Trinity Brompton, London, is recorded as having thought much about the environment or nature—about the problems to which we have all contributed in various ways and the legacy we are leaving for future generations. He believes it should be Christians who are first and foremost in speaking up regarding caring for nature and acting in ways that do this because we, of all people, should recognise that it is the beautiful and wonderful work of God.[48]

Looking after the creation we enjoy so much as an expression of our delight in God is surely one way that we can help fulfil our mandate as new creations in Christ, to live lives that are pleasing to God and that honour Him. This goes hand-in-hand with delighting in the creativity of God and worshipping Him who spoke it all into being and continues to delight in it and sustain it.

Meditation

Does God smile when we delight in the delicate and detailed beauty of a flower? Is He gladdened when we praise Him as Creator of the universe, the forests we walk through and the creatures that abound on this earth? Does He rejoice when we take seriously our mandate to care for that which He has created?

Reflection 14:

The Splendour of
Small Things

Background

The fringe lily (*Thysanotus tuberosus*) is a small, fine native plant that is 20–60 centimetres tall. It flowers in spring or early summer and is found throughout many regions of Australia. The flower and buds of this particular lily were photographed beside a walking track in a local reserve in Newcastle, New South Wales, in late spring. The mauve flowers have three broad fringed petals, alternating with three narrower sepals (modified leaves at the base of the flower that protect the developing flower), which are 12–15 millimetres long. Each flower lasts one day, opening early in the morning and usually withering by early afternoon, but each plant may continue to produce new flowers for several weeks. The species name *tuberosus* comes from the crisp tuberous root. Several tubers, which are 1–2 centimetres long, are produced at the end of the roots. In addition to a wide range of other terrestrial orchid species, Indigenous Australians seek out the edible tubers of these plants as an important source of nutrition.

All living organisms have chromosomes and genes. These chromosomes with their genes make up an organism's genome, which contains all the information needed to develop and maintain that organism. While the genome of this flower has not been studied, we do know that some flowers have a genome up to 50 times longer than the human genome![49] This highlights the incredible hand of God in his design of even the smallest living things, such as native flowers that are often overlooked.

Reflection

When walking through the bush, it may be easy to overlook the small and delicate fringe lily—a tiny patch of mauve amid the grey-greens and browns of native vegetation. Though seemingly insignificant, it is a beautiful Australian example of Jesus' words in Matthew:

> *Therefore I tell you, do not worry about your life, what you will eat or drink; or about your body, what you will wear … See how the flowers of the field grow. They do not labour or spin. Yet I tell you that not even Solomon in all his splendour was dressed like one of these. If that is how God clothes the grass of the field, which is here today and tomorrow is thrown into the fire, will he not much more clothe you—you of little faith? So do not worry, saying, 'What shall we eat?' or 'What shall we drink?' or 'What shall we wear?' … But seek first his kingdom and his righteousness, and all these things will be given to you as well. (Matthew 6:25–34)*

In telling us to not worry about everyday needs, not to make them the focus of our lives, Jesus notices and draws the attention of his listeners to the flowers in the surrounding countryside: '*see how the flowers of the field grow.*'

He then proceeds to make a key point about them: '*they do not labour or spin. Yet I tell you that not even Solomon in all his splendour was dressed like one of these.*' The tiny fringe lily, with its delicate design and mauve beauty, also reflects a splendour that is built into its complex DNA and does not come from human hands.

Jesus goes on to say, '*if that is how God clothes the grass of the field, which is here today and tomorrow is thrown into the fire, will he not much more clothe you—you of little faith?*' (Matthew 6:30). The beautifully adorned, tiny native lilies are not purposefully thrown into the fire, but each flower only lasts one day before withering! As the Creator behind such lovely wildflowers, which, despite their careful fashioning, are so transient, Jesus is saying that we can trust the God whose handiwork they are. If He clothes so carefully such small works in His creation, that last only one day, then is He not more than capable of meeting the material needs of we who are made in His image and very dear to His heart? This does not mean that we are not to work nor support those in need. The provision of work may be a way in which God meets our needs and those of others. Jesus' point is that God can be wholly trusted to care and provide for us and to live out such trust is the very counterpoint to being anxious or preoccupied with such things.

In continuing, Jesus reiterates, '*so do not worry … [about daily needs] … your Father knows you need them. But seek first his kingdom and his righteousness and all these things will be given to you as well.*' Statements that use 'but' are significant; here, the construction highlights Jesus' other key message to us—to centre our lives on God's governance and his justice.

Prayer

Reflection 15:

Life-Giving Water

Background

On the upper reaches of the Paterson River in Barrington Tops National Park, New South Wales, are a series of refreshing waterfalls such as this one. It is without question that water is integral to life on earth.

To better understand the critical role of water in supporting life, it is helpful to see how its structure and properties contribute to this fact. As a simple molecule (H_2O), water is made up of two small, positively charged hydrogen atoms and a larger negatively charged oxygen atom. When the atoms are combined, there is a charge differential between the positive (H_2) and negative (O) parts of the molecule. This differential (or polarity) influences how water molecules interact with each other and with other molecules. For example, as opposite charges attract each other, the positive hydrogens of water molecules 'bond' with the oxygen atoms of adjacent water molecules. This 'sticking together' or cohesion of water molecules explains 'clumps' of water on leaves and other surfaces. Further, this cohesive property of water molecules helps trees to take up water and minerals through their roots and distribute them via the hollow water-conducting cells of the xylem to their uppermost leaves against gravity—an incredible feat for an 80-metre tree, for example.[50]

Some other unique properties of water are (i) its ability to dissolve and transport a wide range of nutrients within organisms; (ii) its critical role in a range of essential biochemical processes, such as respiration; (iii) its capacity to absorb large quantities of heat without significant changes in temperature, which, in turn, helps organisms to regulate their body temperature more effectively; and (iv) the ability of water molecules to move further apart when frozen, becoming less dense, with the result that ice floats on water and allows life to continue to thrive under the ice.[51] All of these features enable water to promote, sustain and refresh life.

Reflection

Australians live on the driest continent on earth, one which is often stricken with drought. Indeed, in recent years, parts of Australia experienced one of the worst droughts on record. Several rural communities ran out of water, and water use was restricted in major cities. We became increasingly aware of how precious and transforming a gift water is. Lack of water is truly life-threatening; so too, is spiritual drought.

In the gospel of John in the New Testament, water is referred to in several chapters, mostly as a reference to spiritual life. In John 4:1–42, it features in the most unorthodox of situations. We read of Jesus, a Jew, somewhat surprisingly travelling through the region of Samaria on His way north to Galilee. There was a 500-year history of hostility and racism between Jews and the people of Samaria (Samaritans). Therefore, most religious Jews would have avoided the perceived contamination of Samaria by detouring around it. Jesus, however, had a clear understanding of where the worst kind of contamination came from—within, and not from without—and acted accordingly.

It is hot, the middle of the day, and Jesus, seated on Jacob's well, is thirsty. *'Will you give me a drink?'* (John 4:7), he asks of a Samaritan woman who, unusually, has not only come to the well alone but has also done so in the midday heat. Women usually went together to collect water in the cool of the early morning or at sunset—Jesus would have known this. Controversially and quite radically, he accepts water from the bucket of this Samaritan woman, who is likely to be a moral outcast.

The two of them converse, and Jesus offers her some surprising information. Having just received a drink of still well water from this woman, he reveals that he could give her *'living water'* (John 4:10)—fresh, running water. He goes on to say that this *'water will become like a spring of water welling up to eternal life'* (John 4:14). Later, in John (17:3), we are told that 'eternal life' is not a vague, distant forever-after life; rather, it means *'knowing God and Jesus Christ'* and may begin right now.

Jesus was offering this woman neither judgement nor rejection, but rather the gift of truly knowing the God who knew her. The *'living water'* he was offering truly is refreshing and renewing and, in fact, life changing. At that point, though, the woman was puzzled by Jesus' offer and wanted to understand more. Sometime later, in John 4:39–42, we read that *'many of the Samaritans of that town believed in Jesus'*, due not only to the woman's story but also what they had heard for themselves directly from Jesus. They drank the *'living water'*. They accepted Jesus' words and his offer, and they let God in. Their minds, hearts and lives were renewed and transformed.

Jesus continues to offer living water to any of us who recognise our thirst for more than the physical things in life. Have you accepted it from him?

Prayer

Gracious God, we thank you that not only do you completely understand the importance of water in our lives, but you also provide living water that satisfies something that we may not even recognise—the thirst of our soul and spirit for you. Thank you, Jesus, that in offering living water to the outcast Samaritan woman, you reveal that no-one is outside your concern and love. Help us to be people who drink your living water gratefully and let you transform our lives so that, in turn, others can be blessed. Amen.

Reflection 16:

Even the Finest Detail

Background

Do you recognise the beautiful detailed 'eye' patterns in the tail of a male peacock? It is thought that the more eyespots and the bigger the tail, the better the chances of the male securing a mate.

One amazing feature of birds is the incredible diversity of colours in their feathers. Where do these colours come from? According to the National Audubon Society,[52] dark colours like blacks and browns come from melanin, the same pigment that contributes to our own hair and skin colour. Melanin is strong; unsurprisingly, it is common in the wing and tail feathers of many bird species. Other pigments made by the bird, such as porphyrine, contribute to the bright red and green colours, particularly those seen in many of our Australian parrot species. However, some colours are not from pigments made by the bird, but from a group of pigments (carotenoids) produced by the plants and algae that are consumed by birds and then broken down and deposited in their feathers and elsewhere. These contribute to warm colours such as oranges and pinks. For example, flamingos are born a dull grey colour and gain their pink colouring from eating algae and crustaceans, illustrating the statement 'you are what you eat'. Conversely, some cooler colours and iridescence come not from pigments but incredibly intricate and detailed feather micro-structures. These are based on a protein called keratin that acts as a prism. It scatters the longer light wavelengths and reflects shorter ones to emit dazzling arrays of colours such as the blues, violets, purples and greens in the 'eyes' of the peacock tail. As the viewing angle changes and the light conditions vary (e.g., from sun to shade), there is a noticeable change in the colours. How incredible is God's attention to detail in this beautiful, diverse part of His creation—birds and their feathers.

Reflection

The exquisite detail and structural composition of the feathers that 'house' the male peacock recall another structure, the design and exact details of which were also planned by God. As Moses led the Israelite families, newly liberated from living as slaves in Egypt, on their journey to the place that would become their homeland, God revealed to him the blueprint for a new structure. This structure was called the 'tabernacle' or 'tent' and was befitting a people on the move and requiring portable dwellings. The blueprint for the construction of the tent included the exact measurements of the structure, the very materials and colours to be used and the designs of the garments and implements used by those serving in it. All are recorded in 15 chapters in the book of Exodus (25–33; 35–40). The purpose of this detailed and precisely designed 'tent' was to signify God's presence with His people, revealing Himself as neither distant nor unknowable, but rather relational and communicative. He graciously came to be present with the people He had rescued in the structure He had designed.

After the Israelites had well and truly settled in their new homeland, God gave another highly detailed plan to their king, David. This plan was for the construction of a more permanent structure for worship—a temple. As a man who had fought many battles, King David was not actually allowed to build the temple, and the plans were passed on to his son Solomon, a man of 'peace and rest' (1 Chronicles 22:9). The seven-year construction process is described in 2 Chronicles 2–7. God declared to Solomon that he had 'chosen the temple as a place for sacrifices and that his eyes would be open and his ears attentive to the prayers offered in that place'. First and foremost, the temple was a place where a relationship with God was maintained through the worship of Him and communication with Him in prayer.

The days of a human-built temple to signify God's presence or as a place of worship are long since gone. Today, true worship comes from perhaps the most intricately designed and remarkably detailed 'structure' of all—the human body—'so *fearfully and wonderfully made*'. It was Jesus who first referred to his own body as a 'temple' (John 2:21). Later, the radically transformed Paul wrote in 1 Corinthians 6:19 that the Spirit of truth lives in the body of the person who believes in Jesus: '*do you not know that your bodies are temples of the Holy Spirit, who is in you, whom you have received from God?*' As temples of the Holy Spirit, our bodies are to be places where God is honoured and worshipped, where, when we draw near to God, He draws near to us and where His Spirit speaks to us truth from God. How awesome is this—the living God meets us in the 'temple' of our bodies that He has so incredibly designed and from which we can worship in Spirit and truth.

Prayer

Holy Father, over the centuries you provided the careful design of structures where people could meet with you. What an extraordinary privilege that now you regard our bodies that you have intricately woven together down to the finest detail as temples for you and where you gift us with the presence of your Holy Spirit. Show us how we should live as people whose bodies are the place of your holy presence. Grant us the deep desire to hear and follow the voice of your Spirit within us amid the din of everyday life. Amen.

Reflection 17:

The Wind Blows

Background

North of Newcastle, between Stockton and Birubi Beach, lies an expanse of ever-changing sand dunes. These dunes, known as the Stockton Bight Sand Dunes, date back 1,100 years. They stretch for 32 kilometres and cover an area of approximately 4,200 hectares. They are the largest living sand dune system in the southern hemisphere, moving at a rate of approximately four metres per year. They comprise a significant part of the Worimi Conservation Lands. The Worimi are the traditional custodians of these lands, which for tens of thousands of years have provided them with food and places to live.

Sand dunes are asymmetrical in shape—the side facing inland (the slipface) is generally at least twice as steep as the windward side and up to 100 metres high.[53] As such, they form a natural defence against the sea and inland erosion. They are also home to incredibly fragile ecosystems of plants and animals that are specialised for such dry, ever-changing environments.

What a joy to arrive at the dunes just before dawn and watch the rising sun transform them from grey masses to rounded mounds of textured pink and golden hues! In the brightening light, a whole new world appears. As we look down, the sand reveals both the delicate and the more substantial imprints of the nocturnal visitors whose tracks have crisscrossed it. Looking up, we see the crests and slopes of the dunes, where varied shapes and patterns created by the elements are displayed.

The smooth, curved forms and the more intricately carved ripples in this photograph caught our attention. They reflect the sculpturing effect of the wind blowing across the dunes, creating patterns and fashioning shapes. These may not have been there a day or days before, and could well be gone the next; however, in the intervening time, they captivate the imagination.

Reflection

This work of the wind recalls the words of Jesus in John's Gospel, Chapter 3:5–8:

> I tell you the truth, no one can enter the kingdom of God unless they are born of water and the Spirit. Flesh gives birth to flesh, but the Spirit gives birth to spirit. You should not be surprised at my saying, 'You must be born again.' The wind blows wherever it pleases. You hear its sound, but you cannot tell where it comes from or where it is going. So it is with everyone born of the Spirit.

These verses are part of a nocturnal conversation between Jesus and a man named Nicodemus. Nicodemus, as a member of the Jewish council, had responsibility for interpreting and implementing Jewish law and rules. Jesus tells him, however, that he cannot enter God's kingdom by obeying the law and rules. Entry comes by the renewing work of the Holy Spirit. Jesus likens this 'work' to the wind, which in those days was a more mysterious element. In other words, Jesus was telling Nicodemus that although he had control over the law (and judgements based on the law), the work of the Holy Spirit, as with the wind, was not something he could control.

C. S. Lewis, the British academic who first became a believer in God and then a believer in Jesus Christ, admits to coming to God 'kicking, struggling, resentful'.[54] He finally felt that he had no choice but to believe. The Spirit of God had been working in his heart and mind. In time, Lewis came to see this persistent work of the Spirit as evidence of God's humility, love and mercy, which had never given up on him. God's Spirit blowing into his life brought Lewis to a place of true freedom and joy.[55]

While the work of the Spirit cannot be controlled by humankind, we read in Luke 11:13 that 'if you then, though you are evil, know how to give good gifts to your children, how much more will your Father in heaven give the Holy Spirit to those who ask him!' In response to His disciples requesting that He teach them to pray, Jesus teaches that God responds to those who ask with the best gift of all—the Holy Spirit. Jesus says, you have asked, and God will give the Holy Spirit. How does that address the disciples' desire to learn to be those who pray? In Romans 8:26–27, we read that the presence of the Holy Spirit 'helps us in our weakness. We do not know what we ought to pray for, but the Spirit himself intercedes for us through wordless groans. And he who searches our hearts knows the mind of the Spirit, because the Spirit intercedes for God's people in accordance with the will of God.'

What a privilege it is to have experienced 'the blowing of the wind'—God's Spirit—in our life. Similarly wonderful is the promise that anyone who seeks God will find Him and anyone who asks will be given the good gift of the Holy Spirit, who knows the mind of God and mediates in our prayer life.

Prayer

Father God, just as the wind blows and shapes the landscape, we thank you for the work of your Spirit throughout this world—blowing into people's lives and bringing about transformation. May we not be people who stifle the work of your Spirit but rather who join in the Spirit's light-, love- and hope-bringing work in this world. Amen.

Reflection 18:

Creation Groans

Background

'Wow, what is it?'; 'Look at all those fish'; 'Is that a shark in there?'; 'Isn't that amazing!' These are some of the responses that this photo engenders.

This huge school of large Eastern Australian salmon (*Arripis trutta*), numbering in the thousands and moving slowly en masse along the Central Coast, was photographed with a drone. The salmon schools move with the Eastern Australian Current and feed mostly on smaller pelagic baitfish, such as pilchards and anchovies.

Rather than a shark, a lone Australian fur seal (*Arctocephalus pusillus*) was enjoying the laid-on food supply. As a near-apex predator, the seal is a voracious feeder and skilful hunter. Using wave power, its own energy or both, it would rapidly launch forward and zoom into the salmon to snatch a meal that was within reach of its sharp teeth. This seal species was once endangered due to being hunted for its fur; while numbers are now recovering, it is nevertheless vulnerable to disturbance at its breeding sites and commercial fishing operations, particularly those involving nets.[56] The Australian fur seal does not commonly occur this far north; so, to observe it in action in the water, seemingly enjoying the wave rides amid the bountiful supply of fish, was quite a privilege.

On other occasions, we have observed similar-sized schools of salmon through the drone camera. These, too, have been the subject of predation, not by the Australian fur seal but rather by sharks, including the grey nurse shark (*Carcharias taurus*), which is now a critically endangered species on the east coast of Australia, and the great white shark (*Carcharodon carcharias*), which may also prey on seals.

Reflection

Predation is a fact of life in our world. Animal species prey on other animal species to eat and survive, doing this by instinct. Cannibalism and even infanticide can occur in the world of creatures and of humankind. Predation and murder are the very opposite of the order in the world that God originally created. Chapters 1 and 2 in the book of Genesis depict creation as unspoiled and good. However, all of this changed.

In Romans 8:19–22, Paul refers to this when he declares:

> For the creation waits in eager expectation for the children of God to be revealed. For the creation was subjected to frustration, not by its own choice, but by the will of the one who subjected it, in hope that the creation itself will be liberated from its bondage to decay and brought into the freedom and glory of the children of God. We know that the whole creation has been groaning as in the pains of childbirth right up to the present time.

While there is still much that is good and beautiful in the created world, it has been and continues to be adversely affected by human choice. In the first chapters of the Bible, we read of the first human, Adam, rejecting the one boundary that had been set in place in his life of freedom—to not eat from the tree of knowledge of good and evil. His desire to be on par with God and, therefore, to eat the fruit of this tree had dire consequences (Genesis 3:1–6). Not only did he and his descendants become as experienced with evil as with good; in a dramatic way, the whole cosmos was disrupted. Can we fully understand this? In humility, we must say, 'No'; but, as Philip Yancy has stated, it does at least match what we know of reality.[57] So much in this world is not good—pain, suffering, anguish, injustice, cruelty and abuse of every kind towards each other and the rest of creation. Creation is, indeed, 'groaning'.

However, this is not its final state. Paul tells us that, conversely, the complete and willing obedience of Jesus to his Father's rescue plan, and his subsequent drawing of people from all over the world into a restored relationship with God as Father, is paving the way for a new earth and a new heaven. There, the adverse cosmic effects will be reversed, and all of creation will be released from its 'groaning'.

In Isaiah, Chapters 11:7–9 and 65:25, we are given a picture of this. Predator animals sit peacefully with those they would normally hunt. Similarly, vulnerable animals and children live in safety with creatures that would usually threaten them: 'the wolf and the lamb will feed together; the cow will feed with the bear, their young will lie down together; … the lion will eat straw like the ox; the infant will play near the cobra's den.' Predation is gone. This imagery of a completely different order in the created world conveys life as God intended it to be, where emotional and physical pain and suffering are gone, and peace and goodness reign, giving true freedom and security.

However, in the meantime, as is so very apparent, the created world 'groans', awaiting release from its corrupted state.

Prayer

Father God, we do not fully understand the cosmic implications of human choice, but we do see the results. We live in a world that is beautiful but hurting in so many ways. May your goodness reign in us that we might be people who bring heaven to this groaning world. We can only do this in surrender to you. You are good. May your goodness rule. Amen.

Reflection 19:

What about Natural Disasters?

Background

This photo was taken with a small point-and-shoot camera in 2011, when we were undertaking a refresher Indonesian language course in Yogyakarta, Central Java, before returning to Aceh, Indonesia. The high mountain in the background is the 2,910 metre Mount Merapi, the most active volcano in Indonesia and one of the 10 most active in the world. The people in this photo are collecting volcanic rock that came from a dangerous flow of extremely hot lava, volcanic ash and deadly gases—termed a 'pyroclastic flow'. This hard, volcanic rock (basaltic andesite), once collected, is skilfully carved into objects, such as mortars and pestles for grinding spices and other local foods, and sold at markets.

Most of the world's volcanoes (including Mt Merapi) are located at the boundaries between the slow-moving rigid tectonic plates, with the majority occurring around the 'Pacific Rim of Fire'.[58] Within these regions of instability, magma from the upper mantle forces its way towards the surface through areas of weakness, as it is lighter than the surrounding solid rock. The molten rock may pour out through a vent as a lava flow; at other times, there may be a violent eruption because the magma is denser and holds trapped gases under high pressure. When released, the eruption sends hot rocks, ash and gases high into the air.[59] Although it remains challenging to predict when a volcano may erupt, using a range of methods including satellite imaging and analysis of seismic and gas data, authorities were able to predict the 2010 eruptions at Mt Merapi, thereby saving an estimated 10,000–20,000 lives by temporarily moving 300,000 residents away from the predicted danger zone.[60]

Reflection

Many of the reflections in this book have focused on delighting in and enjoying creation because it reflects the incredible creativity and glory of the Creator.

However, this is not to deny that, at times, there is a more devastating side to the natural world. Disasters such as earthquakes, landslides, floods and volcanic eruptions can and do occur. While humans have contributed to some of these, many do not result from human activities. We spent some time in Aceh, Indonesia, after the 2004 tsunami and saw firsthand the terrible impact of this event on people's lives. Scientists agree that the tsunami was triggered by a rupture between two tectonic plates in the Indian Ocean;[61] however, local Acehnese were asking, 'what is God saying to us through this devastation and massive loss of life?' One hundred seventy thousand people lost their life in Aceh.

We are disturbed when natural disasters adversely affect communities; we are saddened by the deep suffering caused by the loss of life. Following the shocking devastation in Aceh, over 950 national and international organisations entered that province to provide support, with billions of dollars donated for emergency relief and subsequent reconstruction—a clear demonstration of the generosity of people from around the world, made in the image of a good and generous God (Genesis 1:27).

Although we do not understand why God allows natural disasters, we can be assured of two things: 'God is good' (Psalm 25:8, Psalm 100:5) and 'God is love' (1 John 4:8). We also know that creation is groaning (Romans 8:19–23); however, there is no Biblical evidence to say that any specific natural disaster in recent times is a sign of God's judgement of a particular group of people.[62]

Indeed, to counter the judgemental view of the religious leaders of his day, Jesus used the example of a recent tragedy of a tower collapsing and killing 18 people (Luke 13:4–5) to demonstrate that this was not because those people were more sinful than others. Rather, Jesus emphasised that we all fail to meet the standard as people made in God's image. Conversely, disasters may be triggers for each one of us to consider what is most important in life. They are reminders of our frail and finite nature, that there are things over which we have no control and that, in the end, death comes to us all and may come unexpectedly.

From another perspective and despite the devastation they cause, some natural disasters can also have longer-term benefits. The eruptions and lava flow from volcanoes like Mt Merapi and others in Java over many centuries have resulted in this island being one of the most fertile regions in the world, supporting a population of over 140 million in an area just over half the size of the Australian state of Victoria. In fact, greater than 80 per cent of the earth's surface is of volcanic origin.[63]

Nevertheless, in times of natural disasters and personal tragedy, we may often wonder whether God really cares. For such times, the words of Martin Luther are helpful, 'when you look around and wonder whether God cares, you must always hurry to the cross and you must see him there'.[64]

Prayer

Heavenly Father, you are greater than all the disasters in this world, and you are love, and you are light. As your children, we do not understand all that happens; we cannot see as you see. Help us to trust you even when we do not understand because you are trustworthy. Help us to be your hands and feet and listening ears at these times when people are suffering. Help us to bring your light and love into these situations when and where we are able. Amen.

Reflection 20:

A New Day

Background

Regardless of whether we are 'larks' or 'owls', whether we are awake to see it or not, dawn is a special time. In late summer, at Putty Beach in the Bouddi National Park, I (Bob) awoke before dawn and walked around to the sandstone cliff at the north of the beach. This cliff is terraced and walker friendly. Each of the 'terraces' has unique textures, patterns and shapes, including depressions. After rain or a king high tide, water can remain in these for some time.

On this particularly clear morning, as the sun rose with a glorious display of orange-pinks and mauves across the horizon, it was a delight to see the colours not only spread across the sky but also beautifully reflected in one of the pools in the textured sandstone. This pool—only minutes earlier a semicircle of dark water against dark rock—was now lit with the promise of a new day.

Where do the beautiful colours of sunrise and sunset come from? These colours are not solid like the blocks of paint in an artist's paintbox. Rather, they stem from three factors: the wavelengths of the light, molecules in the atmosphere and the position of the sun. Different wavelengths of light—red, orange, yellow, green, blue, indigo and violet—make up the sun's white light. The atmosphere, through which the light passes, is comprised of gas molecules and small particles. When the light from the sun hits these, it is scattered. At sunrise and sunset, when the sun is low on the horizon, more atmosphere, meaning more molecules and particles, lies between the sun and the earth. At those times of day, violet and blue light, which have shorter wavelengths, scatter more easily and may disappear. Therefore, at such times, the yellows, oranges, pinks and reds, which have longer wavelengths, become more visible.[65]

Reflection

A new day can signal new hope and a new beginning. The book of Lamentations in the Old Testament is thought to have been written by the prophet Jeremiah. In this book, he passionately pours out his grief and sorrow at the situation in which his country, Judah, and its people find themselves. The country has been torn apart by the assault of enemy nations. However, as Jeremiah says, 'those killed by the sword are better off than those who die of hunger' (Lamentations 4:9) because the survivors face starvation and consequently descend into unimaginable acts: 'with their own hands compassionate women have cooked their own children, who became their food when my people were destroyed' (Lamentations 4:10). It is a horrific picture of devastation and desperation.

In his grieving, Jeremiah turns his mind to God. He who recorded God's words of hope for the people of Israel—'for I know the plans I have for you, plans to prosper you and not to harm you, plans to give you hope and a future' (Jeremiah 29:11)—now, in this book of deep sorrow, declares that 'because of the Lord's great love we are not consumed, for his compassions never fail. They are new every morning; great is your faithfulness. I say to myself, "The Lord is my portion; therefore I will wait for him"' (Lamentations 3:22–24).

This is a hope that does not come by denying or minimising the very real horror of all that is about him. Rather, his hope springs from knowing God deeply. From his knowledge of the nature of God comes the hope that with a new day will come a new outpouring of God's goodness and mercy, as needed for that day.

A read through the chapters of Lamentations reveals the mind of one who not only confronts reality but who also examines the reasons for it. For decades, the nation Israel turned its back on God, His teachings and His promises. Instead, they sought other gods—idols made with human hands—and trusted people other than God. They pursued other ways of living, including sacrificing their children in fire (Jeremiah 7:31;32:35), rather than the ways of compassion and justice that were taught by God (Jeremiah 9:24;22:16). Actions bring consequences, and Israel suffered for the choices it made. However, for Jeremiah, who looked to God, the dawning of a new day brings the opportunity to receive blessings anew from Him. Jeremiah not only believes that God's love and mercies will continue; he further declares:

The Lord is good to those who wait for him, to the soul who seeks him. It is good that one should wait quietly for the salvation of the Lord. (Lamentations 3:25–26)

Patiently trusting and looking to and for God when circumstances totally dictate otherwise is the place to which his relationship with God leads him. He is led to see beyond the immediate circumstances to another and greater reality, which is grounded in the goodness and faithfulness of God. This is a reality that the world would deny, but which gives hope that cannot be taken from those who know and love God—the hope of a new day under the love and mercy and goodness of God.

Prayer

Father, much in life happens because of the choices we make, but there are times when we don't understand why things happen. Show us where we need to repent and make amends, but in those situations we don't understand, strengthen us to walk through these with trust and hope in you. For those Lord, who are struggling to face a new day, may your kindness encourage them and your presence sustain them, giving them hope. Amen.

Reflection 21:

Peace and Tranquillity

Background

The 18-kilometre Toolona Creek circuit in Lamington National Park, Queensland, is a beautiful walk that climbs 360 metres (elevation) past numerous waterfalls in a peaceful subtropical rainforest. This scene above a high waterfall immediately struck us as one of those beautiful, peaceful places in which we wanted to pause, be still and give thanks to God. It is a place that helps refresh and rejuvenate the body, mind and spirit.

Rainforests are wonderful places in which all our senses can respond to the beauty and diversity around us. While rainforests cover less than six per cent of the earth's total surface, they are home to 50 per cent of the earth's plants and animals.[66] They play a critical role in sustaining life on the planet, including the regulation of temperature and weather patterns, and absorbing carbon dioxide from the air, storing the carbon and providing us with oxygen. They are also the source of many items in our homes that we take for granted, including medicines—the 'world's largest pharmacy', which accounts for a quarter of ingredients in modern medicines—and food, such as chocolate and bananas.[67]

In an interesting journey of discovery, author and biologist David Haskell visited the exact same square metre of old-growth Tennessee forest to trace nature's path through the seasons. He did this several times a month over 12 months. In documenting his visits, he brought the forest and its inhabitants to life, explaining the ecosystems that bind together the smallest microbes and the largest creatures.[68] With all his senses gradually awakened, he became aware of the intricate complexity of all that was happening in this square-metre patch of rainforest. God has devised such complexity of interdependent ecosystems, not just for one square metre of forest, but for our whole planet!

Reflection

A lush, green rainforest abounds with tall trees, long twisting vines, natural organic smells, the sounds of birds and running water, colourful fungi, small insects and butterflies, fallen leaves and seeds and delicately perfumed flowers. These special places have so many elements that cannot help but stimulate our God-given senses, bringing enjoyment and appreciation. In such places, and despite the constant yet mostly unseen activity, we can amazingly '*be still and know that he* [the One who created and sustains all the beauty we see around us] *is God*' (Psalm 46:10).

For many people, regardless of spiritual beliefs, rainforests are unique places where they experience a sense of peace and tranquillity. This wonderful feeling of peace and serenity is usually temporary, but perhaps it offers a taste of a greater reality. There is a peace—*shalom*—given by God that is even more life-transforming and enduring, and not dependent on our external circumstances or situation.

Before the ordeal of his pending crucifixion, Jesus' thoughts turned to his disciples, and he sought to reassure them, saying, '***Peace*** *I leave with you, my* ***peace*** *I give you. I do not give to you as the world gives. Do not let your hearts be troubled and do not be afraid*' (John 14:27; emphasis added). This is not the 'peace' that we might normally think of—peace that is marked by absence (e.g., of conflict) or escape (e.g., from stress). On the contrary, Jesus' disciples were about to face what the 'world would give'—accusations, violence, mistrust, loss and grief. Yet, Jesus promised them '*shalom*'—peace that brings an inner quiet and security amid turmoil. This gift of peace comes from a real and personal relationship with him—a peace deepened through a growing surrender of life to his loving presence and guidance. Through the brutal death that he was about to face on the wooden cross and his subsequent resurrection, Jesus, the Prince of Peace (Isaiah 9:6), graciously opened the way for a restored peace between humankind and God: '*Therefore, since we have been justified through faith, we have* ***peace*** *with God through our Lord Jesus Christ*' (Romans 5:1; emphasis added).

I have experienced how wonderful it is to know the peace of sins forgiven and that I can quietly trust God to work out His perfect purposes, even when, from a human perspective, things may appear bleak. Once we hand our lives over to God, no matter how difficult our circumstances, we gain assurance that we are loved by Him, and we can trust Him. In this is *shalom*—reconciliation, wholeness and security—peace within and in relationships without:[69]

You will keep in perfect ***peace*** *those whose minds are steadfast because they trust in you. (Isaiah 26:3; emphasis added)*

Do not be anxious about anything, but in every situation, by prayer and petition, with thanksgiving, present your requests to God. And the ***peace*** *of God, which transcends all understanding, will guard your hearts and your minds in Christ Jesus. (Philippians 4:6–7; emphasis added)*

Prayer

Our Heavenly Father and Creator, I give you thanks for rainforests and other beautiful natural places where we can take time out to relax, be refreshed and experience peace. Above all, I thank you for that perfect peace, even in the middle of testing circumstances, that your Spirit gives us as your children. Now may you, the Lord of peace, give your peace at all times and in every way to those I know and love. Amen.

Reflection 22:

Creation in, through and for Christ

Background

This aerial photograph of local tidal wetlands reveals a complex system comprising networks of waterways, emerging mangrove trees, algae of varying hues, shallows and deeper water, mudflats and a flock of birds.

To the human eye, wetlands often seem to be swampy, mosquito-ridden places of little value. However, there is much more to them than meets the eye. Tidal wetlands are incredibly significant support systems that shelter and sustain a broad diversity of plant and animal life. They are breeding grounds and nurseries for numerous saltwater fish and crustaceans. They are resting and feeding grounds for thousands of migratory shorebirds across the world. In these wetlands, sediments collect, pollutants are filtered, soils are created, nutrients are recycled, and water is purified. They store significant quantities of carbon, help to manage stormwater, protect coastal marine life and present a coastal buffer against extreme weather.[70] They can also be used for recreational activities such as fishing, bird watching, photography and kayaking.

Wetlands are amazing, beneficial places; yet, they continue to be treated as wastelands—places to be drained and converted to serve other 'more important' purposes, such as infrastructure, industrial or housing developments or as dumping places for pollutants.

The Hunter Estuary Wetlands are one of 66 Ramsar wetlands (globally recognised as significant for conserving biological diversity) in Australia. The Hunter Estuary Wetlands support vulnerable and endangered species and significant ecological communities. As an end-destination on the biological superhighway known as the East-Australasian flyway, they provide a habitat for numerous species of shorebirds that migrate from the northern hemisphere each year. While here, these birds must increase their body weight by up to 70 per cent to have sufficient energy to fly the great distances back north.[71] It is incredible to think that northern hemisphere species depend on southern hemisphere habitats for their existence and wellbeing—a further example of interconnectedness on our planet.

Reflection

The Son is the image of the invisible God, the firstborn over all creation. For in him all things were created: things in heaven and on earth, visible and invisible, whether thrones or powers or rulers or authorities; all things have been created through him and for him. He is before all things, and in him all things hold together. And he is the head of the body, the church; he is the beginning and the firstborn from among the dead, so that in everything he might have the supremacy. For God was pleased to have all his fullness dwell in him, and through him to reconcile to himself all things, whether things on earth or things in heaven, by making peace through his blood, shed on the cross. (Colossians 1:15–20)

With forthright clarity, these verses in Colossians reveal both the supremacy of Jesus Christ—he was firstborn over all creation, and all things have been created through him and for him—and his absolute sufficiency—in him, all things hold together and, through him, God was pleased to reconcile all things to Himself. There is nothing that has been created that is more powerful or authoritative than he who was before creation, nor is there anything that cannot be reconciled to God by him.

People readily make negative judgements about wetlands and consequently despoil, destroy, or repurpose them when, in fact, they are vital for nurturing life and protecting the environment. Similarly, judgements are made about the value of the spiritual over the material or the value of the material, particularly in terms of profit, over the spiritual. In some circles, the physical world is seen as being less important than the spiritual and, consequently, it is disregarded or devalued and treated accordingly. For others, the physical world is their everything, and the spiritual is ignored. Yet, this picture of Christ in Colossians paints everything—both the physical (things on earth) and the spiritual (things in heaven)—as having value and worthy of being reconciled by Christ and through Christ to God.

These verses negate the concept of dualism—the separation of the material and the non-material—which originated in Greek thinking and teachings. They taught that the latter has more value than the former. However, in linking Christ as both Creator and reconciler of all things, these verses declare that all things matter—both the physical and the spiritual. Therefore, how we live in this world, encompassing all spheres, is critical. There is no merit in becoming so 'heavenly minded' that we are of little good on this earth; nor is there merit in becoming so focused on the material that we neglect the spiritual dimension of life.

What does this mean for us if we are people of God's kingdom, made in the image of God and being renewed by His Holy Spirit?

'If Jesus is Lord of all the earth, we cannot separate our relationship with Christ from how we act in relation to the earth. For to proclaim the gospel that says 'Jesus is Lord' is to proclaim the gospel that includes the earth, since Christ's Lordship is over all creation. Creation care is thus a gospel issue within the Lordship of Christ.'[72]

Prayer

Lord Jesus, you are supreme in all of creation. It is beyond our full understanding that 'all things hold together in you', but the fact that they do, and that through your death you have reconciled all things to yourself, shows us that all things matter. Lord, increase our understanding and show us how we should act in the light of this as people living in this world and children of your kingdom. Amen.

Reflection 23:

Flowing Water

Background

Spa Pool at Hamersley Gorge in the Pilbara, Western Australia, is a popular place; many visitors have enjoyed swimming in the pool and sitting on the rock ledge directly under the refreshing waterfall. Spa Pool's amazing 'design' reflects the effects of mechanical and chemical weathering and erosion, including the long-term impact of flowing water.

This photo captures the effect and beauty of flowing water on a relatively small scale; however, globally, there is a continual vast movement of water in its three forms—liquid, ice and gas. This is the Water or Hydrologic Cycle. The heat from the sun warms the upper levels of ocean water (which account for 97 per cent of the world's water), some of which becomes water vapour. This water vapour rises to the atmosphere and is complemented by evaporation of land-based water (e.g., from rivers), transpiration from trees and plants and the release of water from volcanic activity. As the water vapour from these combined sources rises, it is cooled at higher levels in the atmosphere and may condense into clouds. When water droplets within the clouds become too heavy to remain in the air, they fall to the earth as either rain, snow or hail. A large proportion of this precipitation falls directly into the oceans and other water bodies; however, some falls on land where it may end up in rivers, streams and lakes, or soak into the soil where it may eventually come to the surface in springs or penetrate down to deep underground aquifers.

This process, which is essential for life on earth, is repeated continuously—the water that falls from the sky as rain or flows up from the ground as springs today could well have fallen last month, last year or even last century—God's great plan for recycling a precious resource!

Reflection

There are many references to life-giving water in the Bible. One of the early books, Exodus, recounts the Israelites' journey out of Egypt, where they had lived for 400 years and, in the latter half of those years, been forced to work as slaves. In their exodus, they travelled across deserts and other regions to the fertile new homeland promised to them by God. Chapter 17 of Exodus records an incident at Rephidim, located on the Sinai Peninsula. The Israelites are traversing desert land and feeling thirsty and very unhappy with their changed and unfamiliar circumstances. Consequently, they are complaining to their leader, Moses, about their situation. Moses, in turn, brings the problem to God, who tells him to go to the rock at Horeb: '*strike the rock and water will come out of it for the people to drink*' (Exodus 17:6). Moses did as God told him, and the Israelites' thirst was slaked. God knew exactly where they should go to receive the much-needed thirst-quenching water.

With this incident in mind, in the New Testament, John (one of Jesus' disciples) records Jesus at the Feast of Tabernacles festival as delivering a passionate invitation relating to water. In John 7:37–38, Jesus says with complete authority, '*let anyone who is thirsty come to me and drink. Whoever believes in me, as Scripture has said, rivers of living water will flow from within them.*' Just as God provided a flow of water from the rock at Horeb for the thirsty Israelites, Jesus says that he is the source of life-giving water for those who thirst for God and genuine life.

Jesus alone is the source of this living water. When a person intentionally goes to him and drinks, the Holy Spirit flows. This has effects within, as his or her mind is renewed. Moreover, if the 'flow' is not blocked, then the effect is also felt in the circles in which the drinker moves. God is good and His Spirit is good; therefore, the effect of this flow of the Spirit of God should be good.

Perhaps, at times, the effect may be imperceptible, and the flow may well meet resistance—within and without. The erosive effects of water flowing over rock are often not seen for years; yet, the water continues to flow from its source and, in the process of doing so, brings about change. Jesus promises that thirst-quenching streams will flow '*if we come to him and drink*'—if we listen to, trust and follow him. All we must do is to 'drink' of the abundance and not dam it up inside but let its effects flow out and beyond us.

A Singaporean man, Kenny Gan, was a heroin user and gang member who had spent time in and out of prison. The influences of those with whom he associated shaped him, imprisoning him within and without. Then, he met Jesus and drank the living water. His life was transformed—he was cleansed and released, and he became someone who could not but speak of the one who had quenched his thirst and who was reshaping his life. He once said, 'either we shape our environment, or our environment shapes us'.[73]

Prayer

Gracious God—Father, Son and Holy Spirit—you have provided the earth with an amazing system of water flow that enables renewal, sustains life and shapes the earth. Likewise does your Spirit work in the lives of those who thirst for and drink from you. May this work continue in and through their lives wherever they are in this world to bring honour to you. Amen.

Reflection 24:

Living in the City

Background

This photo captures the city of Newcastle and part of its coastline in the early morning light. Newcastle's location by the ever-changing ocean is a constant reminder of a Creator who existed long before us. Most locals would agree that the lovely beaches and proximity to the ocean are major contributors to the liveability of this city. Another factor is its size. According to research, Newcastle is close to an optimal size, with a dynamic and creative population.[74]

Green spaces also contribute significantly to the city's beauty and liveability. Green spaces are increasingly being recognised as significant contributors to people's wellbeing in cities. Their benefits include cleaning the air and reducing air pollution, cooling the environment and reducing the ill effects of heat, and providing places to exercise, socialise, relax and grow food.[75] The 'green lungs' of Newcastle, Blackbutt Reserve, is a former coal mine restored to 182 hectares of native bushland with majestic carbon-absorbing trees. One of these, the mighty blackbutt (*Eucalyptus pilularis*), has given its name to this Reserve, which is a green, health-promoting space for all who walk its trails in the cool shade of the forest habitat and enjoy its wildlife exhibits and picnic and playground amenities. Other public parks and gardens, such as King Edward Park and the Foreshore park, as well as those in the suburbs, are much appreciated by residents and visitors alike. Additionally, both community and private gardens play a key role in enabling people to enjoy the beauty of God's creation, relax and interact in social networks.

City living need not be incompatible with respect for and appreciation of the natural elements of our environment. Good, creative urban planning should incorporate both and offer the best of human-made and God-made to a city's residents, thereby enhancing liveability in all its dimensions.

Reflection

While many natural features can make a city liveable, the following verses refer to another and, perhaps, neglected factor:

> Build houses and settle down; plant gardens and eat what they produce. Marry and have sons and daughters; find wives for your sons and give your daughters in marriage, so that they too may have sons and daughters. Increase in number there; do not decrease. **Also seek the peace and prosperity of the city into which I have carried you into exile. Pray to the Lord for it, because if it prospers, you too will prosper**. (Jeremiah 29:5–7; emphasis added)

These words, written over 2,500 years ago in a letter by the prophet Jeremiah, address the Jewish people, including leaders and royalty, captured when Judah was attacked by Babylon in late 598 BC. Following their capture, many of the people were taken to live as exiles in Babylon. In passing on to the people what he had heard from God, Jeremiah did not minimise the reality of the length of their exile. However, speaking to their grief at the loss of their homeland, he told them that God would be there to hear and listen to them. In the land of their exile, they could still live in relationship with Him. Moreover, Jeremiah advised them to live life in their new city in a committed and productive, rather than a half-hearted manner.

This productive life was not just for themselves; they were to 'pray for the peace and prosperity of the city in which they had been exiled'. In other words, by their presence, they were to bring blessing to the city and those who lived within. In turn, this blessing would return to them. It is difficult to pray for a person or place that we hate or resent. The very act of praying to God for the city would influence their feelings about it, nurturing a godly attitude towards it and life among its people.

As followers of Jesus, we are people of the kingdom of God. However, we are certainly not yet in 'the new heaven and new earth', nor are we 'of the world' (John 17:14) or do we 'belong to the world' (John 15:19). Wherever we are living right now, we are in a world that is firmly under the influence of one whom Jesus refers to as the 'Evil One'. We have only to consider the terrible things happening in the world to know that evil is at work on many fronts. However, the world that includes ways that are counter to God and that disregard or intentionally reject Him is no longer our 'home'. In a sense, we too, for a time, are exiles.

Therefore, this instruction from Jeremiah has relevance. We should do whatever we can to ensure the peace and wellbeing of the place where we live. This includes praying for it and may mean engaging in actions and activities that truly reflect God and His values. This may include advocating for an environment that has green spaces, freshwater, sustainable energy and clean beaches, which can enhance life for all.

Prayer

Gracious God, even when your people of old had chosen to defy you and suffer, you offered them hope. You also told them to pray for those who had hurt them. In a foreign state, they were to bring your blessing and goodness. Father, as people who live in communities in a city, town or village, we come to you to ask for the peace and wellbeing of these places and to seek your guidance to live in ways that contribute to peace and enhance the wellbeing not only of our fellow citizens but also our environment. Amen.

Reflection 25:

View from Above

Background

Roebuck Bay, south of Broome, Western Australia, is a spectacular place. The reds of the pindan sand and the turquoise of the water are natural and striking, and this is even more apparent when viewed from above with a drone!

With extensive intertidal zones stretching for kilometres, Roebuck Bay has one of the richest biodiversities of any mudflat in the world—between 300 and 500 species of benthic invertebrates.[76] Among other things, these contribute to this bay being one of the most important sites internationally for over 200,000 migratory shorebirds, which feed on these mud-dwelling superfoods to replenish their fat supplies for their annual flight back to the northern hemisphere. If conditions are favourable, after leaving the area, some of them will not land again until they arrive at their first stopover site in North-East Asia. During the five days (6,000 kilometres) it takes to reach the northern hemisphere sites, these birds will fly non-stop, without eating, drinking or sleeping![77]

In the photo, the two birds circling and looking for fish are not shorebirds but black kites. Is their view from above like ours? It is impossible to know for certain, but what is known from studying the anatomy of eagles' eyes and other related research is that, although their eyes are similar in size to the average human eye, key differences include their ability to (i) see simultaneously straight ahead and to the side (a 340-degree field of view, compared to our 180-degree field of view); (ii) see colours more vividly, including ultraviolet light, which helps them to see bodily traces left by their potential prey; (iii) see an ant crawling on the ground from the roof of a 10-storey building or a rabbit over three kilometres away; and (iv) use both monocular and binocular vision, meaning they can use their eyes independently or together, depending on what they are looking at.[78,79]

Reflection

The natural landscape can look so different from an aerial perspective. Likewise, reading the Bible can help us gain a different perspective on our world, ourselves and God. Let us consider three examples.

To reject; to rescue

Genesis, Chapters 37–50, gives us a fascinating story of family discord and God's redemptive purposes. Jealousy drove Joseph's older brothers to remove him from the family. He was sold into slavery in another land, Egypt, where he ended up in prison. People often let him down. However, throughout this whole time, God was with Joseph and his character and skills were being honed for a far greater purpose. As a result of his God-given ability to interpret dreams, and his wisdom and trustworthiness, Joseph was elevated from prisoner to a position of great power. Finally, he was able to see his years of suffering from another viewpoint—that of God. Through Joseph, God not only saved thousands in Egypt from famine but also Joseph's own family and a future nation. This insight enabled Joseph to act with genuine grace and generosity towards his brothers who had so cruelly rejected him: '*you intended to harm me, but God intended it for good to accomplish what is now being done, the saving of many lives*' (Genesis 50:20).

No, we can't; yes, we can!

In Numbers, Chapter 13, we read that God told Moses to send 12 leaders to the land of Canaan to explore the territory he was giving his people. The leaders returned, reporting that '*we went into the land … and it does flow with milk and honey*' (v27)! However, while the 12 leaders saw precisely the same things in Canaan, there was a sharp contrast between the fearful pessimism of 10 of the group, who said '*we can't attack those people; they are stronger than we are*' (v31), and the faithful optimism of the other two, Caleb and Joshua, who said '*we should go up and take possession of the land, for we can certainly do it* (v30) … *If the Lord is pleased with us, he will lead us into that land, a land flowing with milk and honey, and will give it to us*' (Numbers 14:8). Ten saw it through their own eyes (human perspective) and spread negative reports; the other two saw it through God's eyes and knew that they could trust Him to fulfil his promises.

Son of Man; Son of God

As the Son of Man, Jesus interacted with and healed many people. Some viewed him as a prophet, teacher and miracle worker; others saw him as a blasphemer. However, in Luke 9:29–35, on a mountain with Peter, John and James, something extraordinary happened that gave these three disciples a privileged vision of who he really was: '*as he was praying, the appearance of his face changed, and his clothes became as bright as a flash of lightning … they saw his glory … and a cloud appeared and covered them …. A voice came from the cloud, saying, "This is my Son, whom I have chosen; listen to him"*'. As they went up the mountain to pray with Jesus, they had some idea about who he was—the son of man—but, coming down, they had seen his glory as the son of God.

For Reflection

Do my circumstances seem hopeless? Do I need reminding that, 'in all things, God works for the good of those who love him'?

Am I currently resisting the will of God, overcome by obstacles, rather than trusting and obeying him and moving forward?

Am I limiting Jesus by my restricted understanding of who he is—much more than a good man, teacher and prophet—but God?

Reflection 26:

Beauty — Temporary and Everlasting

Background

The sun orchid (*Thelymitra pauciflora*), photographed in bushland on the Central Coast, and the nodding greenhood orchid (*Pterostylis nutans*), photographed in a local reserve in Newcastle, are unique and delicate Australian native ground orchids. Their beauty is unmistakable. Yet, if evolution were the whole story and the efficient functioning of species all that matters, why would so much energy be wasted on developing beauty?

Most of us love the sight or perfume of flowers. Throughout history, artists have painted them—Van Gogh's *Sunflowers* and Monet's *Waterlilies* immediately come to mind. Music has been written about flowers—Tchaikovsky's *The Waltz of the Flowers* or Delibes' *Flower Duet*. Flowers have also formed the subject of poems and books. Moreover, humans across the world 'say it with flowers'. Why? According to Allan Armitage, Emeritus Professor of Horticulture at the University of Georgia, flowers satisfy a need for the basics in life. He believes that love and beauty are elements of those basics, and flowers are so often an expression of both.[80] The beauty of flowers can transform our environment and our mood—bringing joy, happiness and a sense of wonder.

Flowers are an essential part of nature. University of Michigan psychologists Stephen and Rachel Kaplan have conducted many studies on people's responses to nature. These have shown that people value and benefit from it. Further, according to the Kaplans, human appreciation of nature, which includes flowers, is an innate characteristic.[81] This raises the question—where does this innate characteristic come from? Could it relate to the first humans, made lovingly in the image of God, being placed in a garden with fruit-bearing trees that were '*pleasing to the eye*' (Genesis 2:9) and that produced flowers as signs of the food to come, or is it simply that, being made in the image of God, the Creator of beauty, it is in our nature to respond to beauty?

Reflection

The beauty of flowers delights us; nevertheless, what is without question, is that over time, flowers fade and break down. The beauty of an individual flower does not last forever. There is, however, a beauty that does not fade. In Psalm 96, we read, '*worship the Lord in the splendour (beauty) of his holiness; tremble before him, all the earth*' (Psalm 96:9). As flowers are clothed in beauty, in this Psalm, God is described as clothed in beautiful holiness. Beauty is not usually associated with holiness. The media, for example, says much about beauty but rarely in conjunction with holiness. Perhaps this is a 'renew your mind' concept, a challenge to re-evaluate and re-set our thinking about what constitutes beauty.

What does the '*beauty of holiness*' mean? And why doesn't the beauty of God's holiness fade? It does not fade because we are told that God is unchanging (Psalm 55:19). When He is described as holy, that is what He is always like. To understand the meaning of the '*beauty of holiness*', we can look at its effect. Just as flowers can transform a place or mood, the beautiful holiness of God has the power to transform deeply. It is 'purity', a complete 'cleanness'. We cannot infect God with our impurities; rather, His holiness is so powerful that it reveals what is impure in us. This is illustrated in Chapter 6 of the book of Isaiah. The prophet Isaiah recorded a vision he had of God being worshipped: '*holy, holy, holy is the Lord Almighty; the whole earth is full of his glory*' (v3). Isaiah's response, however, is to declare, '"*Woe to me! … I am ruined! For I am a man of unclean lips, and I live among a people of unclean lips, and my eyes have seen the King, the Lord Almighty*'" (v5). God's holiness caused Isaiah to become so aware of his flawed nature—his own unholiness—that he was distraught. However, he was not left in this state: '*then one of the seraphim flew to me with a live coal in his hand, which he had taken with tongs from the altar. With it he touched my mouth and said, "See, this has touched your lips; your guilt is taken away and your sin atoned for"*' (v6–7). In His holiness, God did not remain aloof from Isaiah, nor has He remained aloof from us. He acted to cleanse Isaiah of his flaws and restore him. Likewise, through the death and resurrection of His son Jesus, God offers us cleansing from sin and has graciously opened the way for us to come into the beauty of His holy presence and fellowship with Him (Hebrews 10:19–22).

As His people, God wants us, too, to be holy: '*as obedient children let yourselves be pulled into a way of life shaped by God's life, a life energetic and blazing with holiness. God said, "I am holy; you be holy"*' (1 Peter 1:15–16, The Message). We are encouraged to worship God in the '*beauty of holiness*'; so too are we to live lives which in humility submit to God's good and perfect ways and from which '*the beauty of holiness*' shines. We are to do this both as individuals and collectively as the church.

Prayer

Creator God and our heavenly Father, we thank you for the stunning beauty of flowers that reveal your wonderful creativity and that for a time, bring us so much joy and delight. Help us in our minds and imagination to see your beauty—the beauty of your holiness—and to let it transform us in ways that truly reflect and honour you. Amen.

Reflection 27:

Interdependence in the Deep

Background

One of our favourite activities is snorkelling—to see the 'hidden' beauty of life under the sea. Even though we may go to the same location several times, what we see is always different and mesmerising, whether it be an array of fish whose shapes, colours and patterns reflect seemingly infinite creativity, the graceful and purposeful movements of rays and turtles or the unique and fascinating giant clams (*Tridacna gigas*)—these we had the privilege of viewing while snorkelling during a visit to family in Samoa. The ocean is alive with an amazing array of extraordinary creatures—both seen and unseen.

While each of these underwater creatures is remarkable in its own way, many of them also co-exist with other species in essential relationships. One of these is the giant clam (in the adjacent photograph). This bivalve mollusc can live for over 100 years and weigh over 200 kilograms. These clams could never grow to this size simply through filter-feeding on plankton and other particulates that they draw in through an opening in their mantle—one of the two holes in the soft tissue between the hard shells. Rather, they live in a win-win—or symbiotic—relationship, where they obtain a greater food supply via another organism. In this case, the other 'organism' is millions of photosynthetic algae that live within the clam's mantle (the coloured cells in the mantle). For its part, the clam has specialised cells—known as iridocytes—that help to create an incredibly efficient solar energy harvesting system for the algae to produce food. In return, the algae have a safe place to live and access to the correct quantity of sunlight for photosynthesis.[82] This relationship between the clam and the algae is both interdependent and fruitful.

Reflection

Symbiosis demonstrates the significance of relationships between living creatures and organisms. The algae and the giant clam, co-existing in the saltwater environment of the ocean, need both each other and their environment. Without each other, they would not thrive and, when taken from their saltwater environment, they die. Similarly, humankind thrives best in an environment of love and in relationship with our Creator, God—the Father, Son and Holy Spirit:

As the Father has loved me, so have I loved you. Now remain in my love. If you keep my commands, you will remain in my love, just as I have kept my Father's commands and remain in his love. I have told you this so that my joy may be in you and that your joy may be complete. My command is this: Love each other as I have loved you. Greater love has no one than this: to lay down one's life for one's friends. You are my friends if you do what I command. I no longer call you servant because a servant does not know his master's business. Instead, I have called you friends, for everything that I learned from my Father I have made known to you. You did not choose me, but I chose you and appointed you so that you might go and bear fruit—fruit that will last—and so that whatever you ask in my name the Father will give you. This is my command: Love each other. (John 15:9–17)

In an intimate conversation with his disciples before his death, Jesus spoke to them about environment and relationship. Love is the environment in which they are to live and breathe and have their being. This was love that looked up to God and out to others, like the self-emptying and self-sacrificing love of Jesus for them. It is in this love they are to remain—to intentionally immerse themselves and live out their lives transformed by it.

Further, just as Jesus in John 4:34 stated that '*his food was to do the will of him [God the Father] who sent him*', so he tells his disciples to keep his commands—to do his will. This would be an expression of their love for Jesus and keep them alive in his love. Just as doing his Father's will was fully satisfying for Jesus, doing the good that Jesus asked of them would be the 'food' for his disciple friends. However, this was by no means a one-directional relationship. Jesus wants his friends to know and share his joy—the joy that flowed from knowing God, his Father, intimately, and from doing His will and bringing Him glory. Jesus also shared all that his Father revealed to him with his disciple friends. He did not hold anything back. They were given wonderful insights into the true character and purposes of God, Creator and Lover of humankind.

This close relationship of God the Father, Jesus and his disciples would be fruitful. As Jesus' disciple friends live in this relationship that is outworked in obedience, filled with joy, guided by teachings from God and which was formed and now exists in an environment of poured-out love, it would be productive in and for the kingdom of God.

And so is it for us as Jesus disciples. We, too, are to flourish in Jesus' deep and immense love for us, joyfully doing his will, guided by the Spirit of truth and, in so doing, having an impact for God that will not be erased.

Prayer

Guide us, Lord Jesus, into that deep relationship with you that delights to know and do your will and bring you glory. Amen.

Reflection 28:

Mighty and Majestic

Background

On the steep hike up to Mueller Hut in the Mount Cook/Aoraki National Park, New Zealand, the views are spectacular. In this photo, mountain features can be seen, such as one of the Sealy Tarns, Mueller Glacier, with its lateral moraine, the Hooker Valley and majestic Mt Cook/Aoraki.

Mountains have long fascinated many people, including explorers, bushwalkers, climbers, photographers and artists. They are not static but are continually being transformed by strong forces, including uplift and erosion. For example, while Mt Cook/Aoraki is gouged by glaciers and storms each year, due to tectonic forces, it is also being uplifted by approximately 10 mm per year.[83] Mountains affect weather systems and are critical for life, providing most of the world's freshwater and harbouring a rich variety of plants and animals.

Central to mountain formation is the movement of a small number of large tectonic plates that make up the earth's outer shell or lithosphere—that is, the earth's crust and upper parts of the mantle. This movement is driven by convection currents of molten rock in the mantle. Most geological activities, including volcanoes, other mountain-building processes and earthquakes, occur at the boundaries or intersections of these plates.

Someone who loved being in the mountains was John Muir, also known as 'John of the Mountains' or the 'Father of [USA] National Parks'—a follower of Jesus who spent many years exploring and writing about God's natural world. In his book, *The Mountains of California*, he wrote:

'Climb the mountains and get their good tidings. Nature's peace will flow into you as sunshine flows into trees. The winds will blow their own freshness into you, and the storms their energy, while cares will drop away from you like the leaves of Autumn. As age comes on, one source of enjoyment after another is closed, but nature's sources never fail.'[84]

Reflection

'Purposes, plans, and achievements of men may all disappear like a cloud upon the mountain's summit; but, like the mountain itself, the things which are of God shall stand fast for ever and ever.' (Charles Spurgeon [1834–1892])[85]

As the lands of the Old and New Testaments are quite rugged, it is perhaps unsurprising that mountains and hills are mentioned over 550 times in the Bible. Besides geographical references to mountains where an event or action occurred, mountains are significant in illustrating the attributes of God or as special places where people have had significant encounters with God.

As we spend time near or in the mountains, or simply gaze on a photo of mountains, we might like to remember some of these verses with their truths about God and the journey of faith.

Mountains point to God's incomparable power and might

Who has held the dust of the earth in a basket, or weighed the mountains on the scales and the hills in a balance? (Isaiah 40:12)

You answer us with awesome and righteous deeds, God our Savior, the hope of all the ends of the earth and of the farthest seas, who formed the mountains by your power, having armed yourself with strength. (Psalm 65:5-6)

Mountains are used to illustrate God's steadfast love and protection

As the mountains surround Jerusalem, so the Lord surrounds his people both now and forevermore. (Psalm 125:2)

Though the mountains be shaken, and the hills be removed, yet my unfailing love for you will not be shaken nor my covenant of peace be removed, says the Lord, who has compassion on you. (Isaiah 54:10)

Mountains are places where unique encounters with God occur

After six days Jesus took Peter, James and John with him and led them up a high mountain, where they were all alone. There he was transfigured before them. (Mark 9:2)

Mountains, in their isolation, can be a great place to pray

One of those days Jesus went out to a mountainside to pray, and spent the night praying to God. (Luke 6:12)

Mountains are used as illustrations for teaching truths for Christian living

Truly I tell you, if you have faith as small as a mustard seed, you can say to this mountain, 'Move from here to there', and it will move. Nothing will be impossible for you. (Matthew 17:20)

In looking to the mountains, let them serve as a reminder of who and how great God is, of what He teaches us and to enjoy them as part of His ongoing creative work.

Meditation

He who forms the mountains, who creates the wind, and who reveals his thoughts to humankind, who turns dawn to darkness, and treads on the heights of the earth— the Lord God Almighty is his name. (Amos 4:13)

Reflection 29:

Journey to the Centre of the Earth

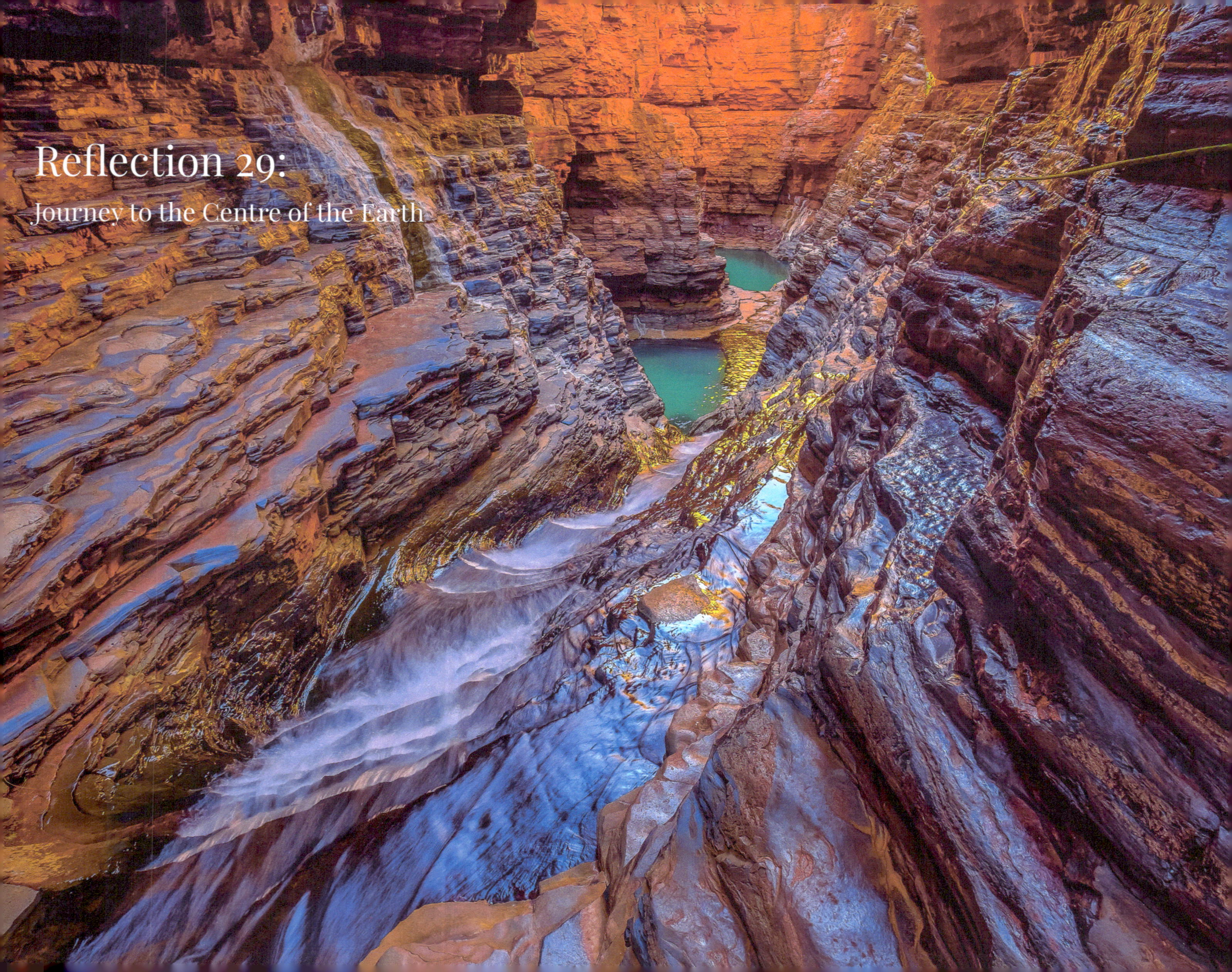

Background

Karijini National Park in the Pilbara, Western Australia, is a popular destination for nature lovers, adventurers and photographers from Australia and overseas. The Park is dissected by breathtaking, deep red gorges and peaceful tree-lined rocky watercourses.

When visiting Karijini National Park, it is possible to join the local adventure company on their 'Journey to the centre of the earth'—an exhilarating 140-metre descent in a Class 6 restricted area to some of the oldest exposed rocks on earth, at the base of Hancock Gorge. The ancient rock is banded ironstone. The dark bands are comprised of iron oxide and silica that was deposited when the atmosphere was low in oxygen and when volcanic activity caused the sea to become rich in iron. The iron reacted with the oxygen produced by cyanobacteria in the upper sunlit levels of the ocean to form iron oxides. The lighter layers in the rock are mostly silica, deposited when the iron content in the ocean was low. Layer upon layer was built up over time, creating banded iron formations that have resulted in the Pilbara region of Australia being so rich in iron. Following a sharp drop in sea level, rivers eroded the areas of weakness to create the amazing steep-sided gorges.

The supervised descent of Hancock Gorge involves challenges such as a high cliff traverse with ropes, an abseil down a rock face and the roped descent of a steep, slippery waterfall. Consequently, some people who undertake this trip and who have not rock-climbed before are initially very frightened; but, by the end, they are thrilled with what they have seen and accomplished. How often is this the case? Overcoming our fears and pushing beyond our limits both surprises and delights us.

Reflection

The challenges we may face in exploring otherwise inaccessible parts of God's creation are small in comparison to what many followers of Jesus face in their journey with God as they walk faithfully with Him. There are numerous examples of this throughout history and until the present day. One example from the New Testament is the second missionary journey of the Apostles Paul and Silas (Acts 15:36–18:22). This three-year journey involved visiting existing churches and establishing new churches. In reflecting on their journey, we can gain valuable insights:

Paul and Silas were guided in their journey by the Spirit of God, through a consideration of what He was saying. This included both negative messages, such as being barred by the Spirit from entering Asia (Acts 16:6f), and positive messages, as with the visionary call to go to Macedonia instead of Bithynia (Acts 16:9f). God is the master strategist and, in our journey with Him, we can trust His guidance and plans. Simplistically, this can be likened to people at Karijini entering Class 6 areas—they need to fully commit themselves to the plan developed by the guides: 'do not go that way, it is too dangerous … Over here, this is the route we need to take'.

Despite the clear guidance of God to go into Macedonia, Paul and Silas faced extreme challenges that threatened their very lives: *'the crowd joined in the attack against Paul and Silas, and the magistrates ordered them to be stripped and beaten with rods. After they had been severely flogged, they were thrown into prison'* (Acts 16:22–23). Following God's clear direction does not mean that we will not suffer hardships and pain—think of what happened to Jesus and to the 70 million Christians who have been martyred for their faith since then![86] We might fall into the trap of thinking that our faith journey with God should be an easy ride—free of persecution, challenges and troubles. This is not what God promises, nor was this the experience of Paul or many other faithful people over the centuries. What God does promise is to be with us—to be our close companion through both the easy and difficult times. Often, it is in the most challenging times that we are more conscious and more appreciative of His presence, perhaps because our sense of dependence on Him is so heightened—we find He can be completely relied upon.

Despite the obstacles and their own fear, the faithful response of Paul and Silas to the call of God resulted in God's kingdom coming and growing in people's lives. These included the businesswoman, Lydia, a jailer under whose guard Paul and Silas had been placed, and a synagogue leader, together with their households (16:14–15; 16:29–34; 18:8). Further, communities of Christians were established in Philippi (16:11–39), Thessalonica (17:1–4), Corinth (18:1–18) and Ephesus (18:19–21). In John's gospel, Jesus told his disciples that, if they followed him—in other words, obeyed him—their lives and actions would reflect his character and bring about his purposes. Paul and Silas' life of obedience, not to rules and regulations, but rather in aligning their will with the guidance of the Holy Spirit, is evidence of this. Is obedience to Jesus our priority? Are we unrealistically expecting a smooth ride in a life of obedience?

Meditation

Nothing whatever, whether great or small, can happen to a believer, without God's ordering and permission. There is no such thing as 'chance', 'luck' or 'accident' in the Christian's journey through this world. All is arranged and appointed by God. And all things are 'working together' for the believer's good.[87] (Romans 8:28)

Reflection 30:

Time for Renewal

Background

The close-up photos of bark on the trunks of the common spotted gum (*Corymbia maculata*) in this collage were taken from a few trees in a nearby reserve. We love taking photos of peeling bark during or just after the rain, as the water brings out the natural richness of the colours and enhances the varied patterns. Compare the bottom right-hand photo taken after heavy rain with the adjacent photo of the same bark before rain.

These images reveal that, as the old bark peels away, new bark appears and is often a mixture of shades of green, yellow, red and purple. The trees in a small area may be of the same species and similar age, yet the colours on the trunks of individual trees can vary dramatically.

Why do gums and many other trees shed their bark annually? The growing season for gums is late spring and summer. When they grow, new layers develop under the older, dead bark as the trunk and branches increase in diameter. As the tree grows from the inside, its outer layers expand, and it sheds its old, less-flexible bark to make way for the new bark. For trees such as the spotted gum, this process of expansion results in a new set of 'clothing', with the old, outer layer completely falling away. In many eucalypt trees, this process is highlighted by a colourful display on the trunk as the old bark dries, curls and peels off, revealing new 'skin' underneath.

What contributes to the bright colours of the peeling bark? Research in this area is lacking, but it is likely that the green of new bark is due to chloroplast-containing photosynthetic cells. As these cells age, the chlorophyll breaks down, revealing new pigments in a range of colours and hues, such as purple.

Reflection

Therefore, we do not lose heart. Though outwardly we are wasting away, yet inwardly we are being renewed day by day. For our light and momentary troubles are achieving for us an eternal glory that far outweighs them all. So, we fix our eyes not on what is seen, but on what is unseen, since what is seen is temporary, but what is unseen is eternal. (2 Corinthians 4:16–18)

The outward wasting away that Paul refers to in the above quote is thought to refer to at least our physical body and, perhaps, our minds. I know for myself that, as I age, signs of deterioration are slowly emerging. For example, I must now wear glasses for reading and driving and there has also been a decline in my hearing. Although reasonably fit for my age, I cannot run as far or as fast as I used to, nor carry as heavy a pack when bushwalking. As with Paul, I and many others must acknowledge the reality that, beyond a certain age, we do notice signs of 'wasting away'.

However, with this and other challenges and troubles that may come our way—Paul, for example, faced pressure from without and within, confusion, persecution, physical illness and attacks from others—there is no need to lose heart, to become despondent and discouraged. Rather, amid these, as we continue to fix our eyes on God, on the reality that is unseen and eternal, an inner transformation occurs. We are being constantly conformed to the likeness of Christ and, ultimately, being prepared for living in the glorious eternal presence of God, where there will be no more decay and wasting away of our bodies.

To return to the photos, living a vibrant Christian life can be somewhat like the growth and renewal that occurs with many eucalypts. Annually, the outer bark, some of which may have been damaged by insect and fungal attack, is in a state of decay. However, underneath this old bark is hidden new life and renewal. In God's purposeful creation, this new layer of bark, with the input of energy from the sun, is manufactured from water and other nutrients from the soil coupled with carbon dioxide from the air. It is the same with us. Despite our outer body wasting away, as we nourish ourselves on the riches of God, we are continuously renewed within. As with trees, this new growth and renewal are all from God, and it is beautiful in His eyes as we are slowly changed into the likeness of Jesus and prepared for an eternity with him, the Lamb of God who made the ultimate sacrifice. Death, when it comes to us, means the end of the old—of sin and mortality—however, beyond that lies a new life, a restored life, a fresh start in a new and imperishable body.

Meditation

Just as a tree is nourished from within, so too can God work His mystery in us, individually and communally as the church, renewing us within, but we need to work with him to allow this to happen. *His divine power has given us everything we need for a godly life through our knowledge of him who called us by his own glory and goodness. Through these, he has given us his very great and precious promises so that through them you may participate in the divine nature, having escaped the corruption in the world caused by evil desires. For this very reason, make every effort to add to your faith, goodness; and to goodness, knowledge; and to knowledge, self-control; and to self-control, perseverance; and to perseverance, godliness; and to godliness, mutual affection; and to mutual affection, love. (2 Peter 1:3–7)*

Reflection 31:

Tested in the Fire

Background

Among ecologists and botanists, Australia is known internationally for having an amazing array of plants and trees that are well adapted to fire. Many species only release seeds after a fire, whereas others need fire to germinate or flower. Over thousands of years, Indigenous Australians utilised such knowledge in their sustainable use of well-managed fire.

One of the best-known examples of 'new life' after fire occurs with *Xanthorrhoea* species or, as they are better known, grass trees. The photograph reveals the blackened trunks, new growth and flowering spikes of *Xanthorrhoea glauca* at Mt Cabre Bald in Barrington Tops National Park. A fire, which began with a lightning strike in late November 2019 and burned for several months, affected most of this unique and spectacular seven-hectare grass tree forest. Yet, how amazing has been the subsequent recovery of the grass trees, with literally thousands displaying new green leaves and prolific flowering!

In a review of grass tree ecology, Lamont et al. (2004) reported that grass trees are highly flammable—temperatures greater than 1000 degrees centigrade have been recorded in the lower parts of the plant during a fire. This is due to their long thin dense 'skirt' of dead leaves that are not shed but rather accumulate, trailing vertically beneath the green leaves above. However, the growing tip of the plant is sheltered by the surrounding young green leaves. After a fire, the trees, which usually grow just 1–2 centimetres per year, send out spectacular flowering spikes that grow at 10 centimetres per day, often reaching skyward 2–3 metres. Therefore, they are a very conspicuous source of food for pollinators. These flowering spikes, each of which may contain up to 8,000 seeds, are a critical lifeline after a fire, being an excellent food source for species of insects, birds and small mammals.

Reflection

The 'trial' by fire, which enables the grass trees to produce abundant nectar-rich flowers and seeds that serve both the grass trees and other species, illustrates well a theme that is not uncommon in the Bible. This theme is taken up in the letter written by James to the scattered followers of the Way (Jesus).

Consider it pure joy, my brothers and sisters, whenever you face trials of many kinds, because you know that the testing of your faith produces perseverance. If any of you lacks wisdom, you should ask God, who gives generously to all without finding fault, and it will be given to you. But when you ask, you must believe and not doubt, because the one who doubts is like a wave of the sea, blown and tossed by the wind … Blessed is the one who perseveres under trial because, having stood the test, that person will receive the crown of life that the Lord has promised to those who love him. (James 1:2–6 &12)

In these verses in the opening chapter of the book, James juxtaposes two ideas that are not normally linked—'joy' and 'trials'. This is definitely a 'glass-half-full' perspective on the 'trials' that occur either due to what is going on within us or to sources and circumstances beyond us. Times of unexpected testing are often difficult to endure and do, indeed, challenge our faith. We may ask: 'Is God really with us?'; 'Is God really hearing our prayer about this?'; 'Is this ever going to end?'; or 'Will we have the strength to get through it, and what good is it?' It may well feel like God is not with us at such times; yet, as His children, He promises 'never to abandon us' (Hebrews 13:5) and is certainly fully aware of what we are going through. At such times, faith can blossom, or it can wilt.

As James suggests, faith that does not wilt in the testing times perseveres. It continues, '*confident in what is hoped for and assured of what is not seen*' (from Hebrews 11:1). It may only be when we are past the challenge that we can look back with gratitude and see what we have learned and how we have been enabled. In the meantime, James strongly encourages us to see testing times from a 'higher' view—as opportunities in which we should not run away from or give up on God, but rather which we should move through, continuing to trust Him and thereby growing into maturity as new or even not-so-new creations in Christ. Hence the joy, which comes not from a fleeting feeling but from an intentional and grateful heart and mind submitted to the greatness and wisdom of God who '*works for the good of those who love him*' (Romans 8:28).

If we are struggling to do this, then James advises us to 'ask God' for wisdom to see our trials from this perspective and to make up our minds to act accordingly. This, in turn, reflects both our love for God and trust in Him and will be rewarded with life—eternal life, knowing and communing with the living God.

Prayer

Father God, trials are an inevitable part of our life on this earth. As we go through them, we thank you that we can pour out our deepest feelings to you and that as our Father, you hear, you care and you are with us. Through these times, we pray for your strength to persevere in faith. We ask for your wisdom to see the trials as you would have us do so, and we ask that you do immeasurably more than we can imagine and enable us to count them as joy to the glory of your name. Amen.

Reflection 32:

In the Storm

Background

Those who live near the ocean know only too well the power of the strong winds and torrential rain that can lash our coastline. Now and then, we experience these conditions in Newcastle, north of Sydney.

One late afternoon, we walked out along the break wall between Nobby's Beach and Newcastle Harbour to see and photograph the effects of an extreme east coast low weather system. Waves up to 10 metres high were crashing into and over the wall. Not only were those of us who ventured a little too near the end of the wall drenched with the far-flung spray, but the roaring winds continuously drove stinging particles of sand into our faces, hair and clothing. It was a battle to stand still enough to photograph the dramatically awesome scene.

East coast lows are intense low-pressure systems that occur off the east coast of Australia. They can be particularly dangerous, resulting in long periods of damaging winds and rain, big seas and surf that, in turn, often cause extensive coastal erosion and flooding. However, while these weather systems can be very costly for communities, they can also be crucial for restoring river flows and replenishing water storage in dams.

During an east coast low in mid-2007, the Pasha Bulker, a bulk carrier that had been waiting offshore to enter Newcastle Harbour, was driven onto a local Newcastle beach by the wind, waves and currents. It sat there for several weeks, a mighty red-hulled testament to the power of the huge storm that had struck the region. Another east coast low that hit the headlines both here and overseas was one that affected the 1998 Sydney to Hobart yacht race, leading to the deaths of sailors, yachts sinking or having to retire from the race, and numbers of participants requiring rescue by helicopter.

Reflection

An incident that echoes these events is recorded in the book of Acts, Chapters 27 and 28. The Apostle Paul was under wrongful arrest due to actions taken by other Jews who were upset with his ministry. As a Roman citizen, Paul claimed his right to have the case heard in Rome, rather than in Jerusalem; therefore, under the guard of a soldier, he boarded a ship destined for that city. However, early in the voyage, the ship was overtaken by a raging storm that lasted for days.

What insights can we gain from this account of 'the storm'?

Throughout the storm, Paul was trusting, prayerful and caring. As a seasoned traveller, he knew it was not a good time to set sail and made the following prediction: '*men, I can see that our voyage is going to be disastrous and bring great loss to ship and cargo, and to our own lives also*' (Acts 27:10). However, the ship did leave, only to be struck by the relentless storm. Finding his life in danger, in addition to those of the crew and other passengers, Paul kept in touch with God through prayer. He prayed not only for himself but also for the lives of all those he was travelling with. By holding on to a promise that God had given him some time before—'*as you have testified about me in Jerusalem, so you must also testify in Rome*' (Acts 23:11)—and by continuing to listen to God, he received assurance that he and the others on board would survive. He shared this with them to encourage and reassure them: '*but now I urge you to keep up your courage, because not one of you will be lost; only the ship will be destroyed*' (Acts 27:22). He was not only prayerful but also caring, encouraging those aboard to eat some food and renew their strength in preparation for the next phase of the ordeal—an intentional beaching: '*just before dawn Paul urged them all to eat. "For the last fourteen days", he said, "you have been in constant suspense and have gone without food—you haven't eaten anything. Now I urge you to take some food. You need it to survive"*' (Acts 27:33–34).

Shipwrecked on the island of Malta, Paul did not resent being short of his destination, Rome. Instead, he saw their being on the island as part of God's looking after them all, and he maintained a faithful attitude among the kindly locals who took them in. In so doing, he touched their lives in a Jesus-like way: '*his* [Publius, the chief official on the island] *father was sick in bed, suffering from fever and dysentery. Paul went in to see him and, after prayer, placed his hands on him and healed him. When this had happened, the rest of the sick on the island came and were cured*' (Acts 28:7–9).

Storms may arise in our lives over which we have little or no control. They may well be the result of others' decisions. They may be frightening and even overwhelming. Whom do we turn to first in such circumstances? Do we trust God enough to let Him minister to us through the storm that we may, in turn, minister to others?

Prayer

Father God, storms are indeed a part of life, but you are so much greater than any we may encounter. Help us to live in dependence on you, so that when storms do come, you are the first one we turn to and listen for. May it be your wisdom and voice that guide us and may you bring good out of these storms. Amen.

Reflection 33:

Seeing Indistinctly—A Call to Humility and Love

Background

This photo captures a wave breaking in shallow water just after sunrise. I (Bob) purposely used a low shutter speed (1/20 second) to blur the movement of the wave, as part of an exercise to create a series of minimalist photos.

Most people enjoy watching the ocean. There is invariably something interesting to see—the beautiful sunrise and sunset colours on the water, shells and seaweed washed up on the beach, birds diving to catch fish, dolphins cruising along or migrating whales breaching. In addition to these, what we are guaranteed to see, and which appear differently every day, are ocean waves. They give the ocean its 'endless motion', its restlessness.

Most waves are caused by friction between wind and the ocean surface; energy from the wind is transferred to the water, creating a wave crest. These wave crests often combine with others, creating 'sets' of waves. They can travel thousands of kilometres, moving energy from one side of the ocean to the other.[88,89] Although ocean waves transport energy over vast distances, only a small quantity of water moves across the ocean. Rather, water particles within the wave are moving up and down. This can be illustrated by visualising a boat floating on the water. The passing waves do not move the boat towards the shore; rather, the waves move the boat first up and forward, then down and, finally, back to a place near the original position. Neither the boat nor the water moves towards the shore—only the wave form and energy.[90] We think we are looking at the water moving all the way across the ocean to our shore when, in fact, it is energy that is moving in and through the water. Perhaps, waves provide an example of a situation in which we do not see clearly.

Reflection

For now, we see only a reflection as in a mirror; then we shall see face to face. Now I know in part; then I shall know fully, even as I am fully known. (I Corinthians 13:12)

Paul, the writer of this first letter to the church in Corinth, in alluding to the fact that the high-quality bronze mirrors of the day reflected an indistinct image, used this analogy to remind his readers that, as finite people, our capacity to understand God and His ways is limited. God, in His entirety, is too great and too wonderful for us to get our heads around—complete knowledge of God is impossible because, ultimately, He is mystery. However, God does enable us to see partially. In creation, we see the beauty and power, creativity and majesty of God. Additionally, He has given us a book to help us know Him. The Bible tells us much about God and, in Jesus, it shows us what intimacy with Him is like and leads to—setting apart time to listen to and speak with God, acting compassionately to bring hope and justice, challenging misrepresentations of God and His character and teaching to give further insights into God's heart. There is much that we can 'know in part', and it is mind-blowing to think that this is, indeed, just a 'part'.

However, our partial knowledge is not where we stop. According to this same verse, a time will come when everything concerning God will become clear. We will stand 'face-to-face' with the one whose character is multifaceted—holy and loving, just and merciful, king and servant, powerful and gracious, all-wise and compassionate. In the meantime, recognising that we do not and cannot 'know' God perfectly is critical. This is a reminder of our creatureliness—albeit a creatureliness honoured with being made in the image of God—and, therefore, our limitations. It is also a call to faith in God, especially in testing times, when it is particularly difficult to understand the why and the wherefore of certain life events. Accepting that we do not yet see clearly should lead us to a place of humility and, as the broader context of this verse encourages (1 Corinthians 13), to be guided by love in our thoughts, words and actions. This is a call to live our lives humbly and lovingly.

While in our current state, we will never understand or know God fully, the final words of this verse declare the very opposite of God. He fully knows us as His very much loved creation. This is significant as it means we can hide nothing from Him. He knows us completely; therefore, we can enter into a relationship with Him from a position of complete visibility and in an attitude of complete honesty. There is nothing in us that He cannot see or that precludes Him loving us. This is potentially the most liberating and healing relationship to be in—to be humble and transparent and to receive His wisdom and love.

Prayer

Loving Heavenly Father, you are so much greater than all we can see and know. What you have revealed is already amazing. Thank you that a time is coming when we will see you 'face-to-face' in all your glory. In the meantime, may we handle with humility, grace and love the insights you have given us, using them not to bring judgement but blessing. Thank you, too, that you know us completely and that we can entrust ourselves to you to work in us to your praise and glory. Amen.

Reflection 34:

Our Response

Background

On a still morning, sunrise over the water—with the constantly changing colours of a new day dawning—is a captivating sight. This photo was taken as the sun rose over a coral reef gradually being submerged by the incoming tide. The coral lagoon is located on Lady Elliott Island, the southernmost coral cay in the Great Barrier Reef.

Lady Elliott Island is a wonderful example of the effects of creation care. The subtropical island was completely denuded by the mining of guano (bird droppings), and it remained in this barren state for decades. However, it has now been revegetated and restored by a small group of committed people. With the regrowth of a variety of trees and shrubs, the birds, insects and microorganisms returned. It is now a place on the Great Barrier Reef that is rich in both island flora and fauna and marine life.

The restoration of the island flora began in 1969, when pilot Don Adams arrived on the island and began a revegetation program using shrubs and seedlings of native plants from nearby islands and the mainland.[91] Today, the island and surrounding waters which are now a Marine National Park (Green Zone) are home to 250 species of birds and over 1,200 different species of sea life, including manta rays, turtles, humpback whales, sharks and colourful fish.

Not only has the island been restored, but it continues to be managed sustainably with a focus on minimising its carbon footprint and resource usage. The management of Lady Elliot Island is a collaboration of private business, government agencies and services; as such, it works to proactively educate and inspire its visitors and the broader population about our precious and beautiful environment.

Reflection

In the beginning was the Word, and the Word was with God, and the Word was God. He was with God in the beginning. **Through him all things were made; without him nothing was made that has been made** *… The true light that gives light to everyone was coming into the world. He was in the world,* **and though the world was made through him, the world did not recognise him**. *(John 1:1–3;9–10; emphasis added)*

Creation exists first and foremost to bring God glory and joy: '*the heavens declare the glory of God; the skies proclaim the work of his hands*' (Psalm 19:1) and '*how many are your works, Lord! In wisdom you made them all, the earth is full of your creatures … May the glory of the Lord endure forever; may the Lord rejoice in his works*' (Psalm 104:24 & 31). Despite its now tainted condition, creation still reflects the glory of its Creator. We are told that Jesus (the Word) was the agent in that creative process, bringing forth the created world by divine activity and in such a way that it is sustained and regularly renewed. Creation is an extraordinary expression of the triune God. It deserves our wonder and respect.

If creation exists for and reveals the Creator, God (Romans 1:20), does not disregard or destruction of it show dishonour to God and mean that we lose something precious that speaks about Him to all of us? Professor Norman Wirzba wrote that modernity, characterised by scientific thought, industrialisation and individualism, has elevated the self as the giver of meaning to the world, as opposed to our discovering meaning from and in the world around us. This is significant as it feeds into the perception that the natural world exists primarily for our benefit or is an inconvenience to be removed.[92] Its dimension as an expression of an amazing Creator who delights in His creation is ignored. Just as Jesus '*was in the world, and though the world was made through him, the world did not recognise him*', are we guilty of not recognising the hand of God in creation? Are we defaulting to the secular, modern view and missing out 'on the larger meaning of this world in which we live?'[93]

Humankind was placed in creation, but nowhere does it say that creation was made for us. Certainly, plants were to provide food and, after the Fall, most creatures could be eaten, and people could make use of the elements in their environment, like iron and copper (Deuteronomy 8:9), to create objects and art. However, there is wise and considerate use, and there is selfish and destructive use—where do we fit as new creations in Christ?

Nature ultimately belongs to our Father in heaven on whom we and all creatures depend for life. Through the agency of Jesus (the Word), He created such incredible abundance from nothing. Caring for nature—the creative work of the triune God—will first and foremost bring praise to Him and blessing to ourselves, our neighbours, future generations and the world in which we live.

Prayer

Father God, may we honour you as Creator of heaven and earth. Lead us not only to see your extraordinary world and your purposes for it as you do, but grant us the strength of will and character to act responsibly for the glory of your holy name. May your kingdom come for all your creation, and your will be done on earth as it is in heaven. Amen.

Nature is a miracle–unimaginable abundance and diversity, grandeur and detail–wrought from nothing by God as an expression of divine love. It is only right to be awed by it, give praise to God for it and in gratitude, care for it.

Photo: Eastern spinebill feeding on a grevillea, New South Wales, Australia

But he [Jesus] said, "If they [the people] kept quiet, the

stones would do it for them, shouting praise."

(Luke 19:40, The Message)

You are worthy, our Lord and Our God, to receive the glory and the honour and the power, because you have created all things, and by your pleasure they exist and were created.

(Revelation 4:11)

References

1 Steffens, M. (2009, 27 July). *Australia's first astronomers*. ABC. https://www.abc.net.au/science/articles/2009/07/27/2632463.htm

2 Banks, K. (2019). *65,000 years—the great history of Aboriginal astronomy* [video]. YouTube. https://www.youtube.com/watch?v=mYr7ZCn04eA

3 Comer, J. M. (2017). *Garden city: Work, rest and the art of being human*. Grand Rapids, Michigan: Zondervan. (p. 42).

4 Chapman. A. D. (2009). *Numbers of living species in Australia and the world. A report for the Australian Biological Resources Study*. Australian Government: Department of Agriculture, Water and the Environment. http://www.environment.gov.au/science/abrs/publications/other/numbers-living-species/executive-summary#chordates

5 Australian Museum. (2018). *Eastern spinebill*. https://australian.museum/learn/animals/birds/eastern-spinebill/

6 Colwell, M. (2014). John Muir: The Scotsman who saved America's wild places. Oxford, England: Lion Books.

7 Johnson, C., Cogger, H., Dickman, C. (2007). Impacts of land clearing: the impacts of the approved clearing of native vegetation on Australian wildlife in New South Wales. World Wide Fund for Nature.

8 Bush Heritage Australia. (n.d.). *Grass trees*. https://www.bushheritage.org.au/species/grass-trees

9 Watson, P. (2004). *The grass tree: Its uses and abuses*. Australian Plants Online. http://anpsa.org.au/APOL33/mar04-5.html

10 Sanders, A. (2017). *What are the most visible colours from a distance?* Sciencing. https://sciencing.com/visible-colors-distance-8209029.html

11 Comer, J. M. (2017). Garden city: Work, rest, and the art of being human. Grand Rapids, Michigan: Zondervan.

12 Modified from Moo, D. J. & Moo, J. A. (2018). *Creation care: A Biblical theology of the natural world*. Grand Rapids, Michigan: Zondervan. (Kindle Edition, p. 8).

13 Moo, D. (2018). The Epistle to the Romans (The New International Commentary on the New Testament) (2nd ed.). Grand Rapids, Michigan: Eerdmans Publishing Company.

14 National Snow and Ice Centre Data. (2020). *All about glaciers*. https://nsidc.org/cryosphere/glaciers/quickfacts.html

15 Modified from Moo, D. J. & Moo, J. A. (2018). *Creation care: A Biblical theology of the natural world*. Grand Rapids, Michigan: Zondervan. (Kindle Edition, p. 65)

16 Peterson, E. H. (2008). *Christ plays in ten thousand places: A conversation in spiritual theology*. Grand Rapids, Michigan: Eerdmans Publishing Company. (p. 71).

17 Department of Conservation. (n.d.) *Great walks: Routeburn Track*. https://www.doc.govt.nz/globalassets/documents/parks-and-recreation/tracks-and-walks/southland/routeburn-track-brochure.pdf

18 Wikipedia. (n.d.) *Pounamu*. https://en.wikipedia.org/wiki/Pounamu

19 Saint Augustine. (2002). *The confessions of Saint Augustine*. (Original work published 401). https://www.gutenberg.org/files/3296/3296-h/3296-h.htm

20 Orr, J. E. (1936). *Search me, O God*. Based on Psalm 139:23-24. Public domain.

21 Australian Museum (2018, 18 November). *Pollination*. https://australianmuseum.net.au/learn/animals/insects/pollination/

22 Motyer, J. A. (2005). *The message of Exodus in The Bible Speaks Today* (Old Testament set). Nottingham, England: Intervarsity Press.

23 Met Office. (n.d.). *10 striking facts about lightning*. https://www.metoffice.gov.uk/weather/learn-about/weather/types-of-weather/thunder-and-lightning/facts-about-lightning

24 Andrews, K. (2015). *Six striking facts about lightning*. ABC News. https://www.abc.net.au/news/science/2015-12-07/lightning-facts/6993880

25 Atkinson, D. (1996). *The message of proverbs. The Bible speaks today*. Nottingham, England: Intervarsity Press.

26 Roebuck Bay working Group Inc. (2017). *Benthos (mud) monitoring*. https://www.roebuckbay.org.au/volunteer-activities/benthos-monitoring/

27 Piersma, T., Pearson, G. B., Lavaleye, M., Hickey, R., Rogers, D. I., Holthuijsen, S., Marin-Estrella, S., de Goeij, P., Findlay, N. & Storey, A. W. (2016). *Anna Plains and Roebuck Bay Benthic Invertebrate Mapping 2016*. http://globalflywaynetwork.com.au/wp-content/uploads/2016/11/AnnRoeBIM16-the-field-report.pdf

28 Atkinson, D. (1996). *The message of proverbs: The Bible speaks today*. Nottingham, England: Intervarsity Press.

29 Atlas of Living Australia. (n.d.). *Desert death adder*. https://bie.ala.org.au/species/urn:lsid:biodiversity.org.au:afd.taxon:3fa6d6d1-09a3-4b03-8041-f20031434743

30 Sadananda Naik, B. (2017). *'Dry bite' in venomous snakes: A review*. Toxicon, 133, 63–67. https://doi.org/10.1016/j.toxicon.2017.04.015

31 Australian Museum. (n.d.) *Cunjevoi*. https://australianmuseum.net.au/learn/animals/sea-squirts/cunjevoi/

32 Timeless Truths, Free Online Library. (n.d.). *The old rugged cross—George Bennard*. https://library.timelesstruths.org/music/The_Old_Rugged_Cross/

33 Timeless Truths, Free Online Library. (n.d.) *The old rugged cross—George Bennard*.

References

https://library.timelesstruths.org/music/The_Old_Rugged_Cross/

34 Timeless Truths, Free Online Library. (n.d.). When I survey the wondrous cross—Isaac Watts. https://library.timelesstruths.org/music/When_I_Survey_the_Wondrous_Cross/

35 Birdlife Australia. (n.d.). *Powerful owl*. http://www.birdlife.org.au/bird-profile/powerful-owl

36 WIRES: Land for Wildlife Notes. (n.d.). *Tree hollows for wildlife*. https://www.wires.org.au/wildlife-info/wildlife-education/tree-hollows-for-wildlife

37 Victoria Department of Natural Resources and Environment. (1999). *Wildlife needs natural tree hollows*. https://www.swifft.net.au/resources/6_wildlife%20needs%20natural%20hollows.pdf

38 Chambers, O. (1963). *My utmost for his highest: 5 August*. Ohio: Barbour Publishing.

39 University of East Anglia. (2018, 6 July). *It's official—spending time outside is good for you*. ScienceDaily. www.sciencedaily.com/releases/2018/07/180706102842.htm

40 American Heart Association. (2018, 1 August). *Spend time in nature to reduce stress and anxiety*. https://www.heart.org/en/healthy-living/healthy-lifestyle/stress-management/spend-time-in-nature-to-reduce-stress-and-anxiety

41 New York State Department of Environment and Conservation. (n.d.). *Immerse yourself in a forest for better health*. https://www.dec.ny.gov/lands/90720.html

42 Florida Health (2018, 28 June). *5 health benefits of spending time in nature*. http://www.floridahealth.gov/newsroom/2018/06/062818-article-5-health-benefits-of-spending-time-in-nature.html

43 Rook, G. A. (2013). Regulation of the immune system by biodiversity from the natural environment: an ecosystem service essential to health. *Proc Natl Acad Sci U S A. 110(46):18360-18367. doi:10.1073/pnas.1313731110*

44 Merriam-Webster Dictionary. (n.d.). Delight (n). In *Merriam-Webster Dictionary*. https://www.merriam-webster.com/dictionary/delight

45 Dictionary.Com. Unabridged. (n.d.). Delight. In *Dictionary.com*. https://www.dictionary.com/browse/delight

46 Merriam-Webster Dictionary. (n.d.). Delight (n). In *Merriam-Webster Dictionary*. https://www.merriam-webster.com/dictionary/delight#synonyms

47 John, E. (2018). *Interview: Richard Powers: We're completely alienated from everything alive*. The Guardian. https://www.theguardian.com/books/2018/jun/16/richard-powers-interview-overstory

48 Ware, J. (2015, December). Premier Christianity. https://www.premierchristianity.com/Past-Issues/2015/December-2015/Environgelicals-reclaiming-environmentalism-from-the-New-Age-movement

49 Royal Botanic Gardens, Kew. (2010, 7 October). *Rare Japanese plant has largest genome known to science*. https://www.sciencedaily.com/releases/2010/10/101007120641.htm

50 Sargen, M. (2019, September 26). *Biological Roles of Water: Why is water necessary for life?* SITN: Harvard University. http://sitn.hms.harvard.edu/uncategorized/2019/biological-roles-of-water-why-is-water-necessary-for-life/

51 Pidwirny, M. & Gow, T. (n.d.). *Land Use and Environmental Change in the Thompson-Okanagan*. https://royalbcmuseum.bc.ca/exhibits/living-landscapes/thomp-ok/env-changes/water/introduction.html

52 Goldman, J. (2016, 4 March). *What makes bird feathers so colorfully fabulous?* Audubon. https://www.audubon.org/news/what-makes-bird-feathers-so-colorfully-fabulous

53 Alpha, T. R., Galloway, P. & Starratt, S.W. (1998). Sand dunes: Computer animations and paper models. US Department of the Interior. US Geological Survey. https://pubs.usgs.gov/of/1998/0131a/report.pdf

54 Lewis, C. S. (1977). *Surprised by joy*. Glasgow: William Collins Sons & Co.

55 Lewis, C. S. (1977). *Surprised by joy*. Glasgow: William Collins Sons & Co.

56 Australian Museum. (2019). *Australian fur seal*. https://australianmuseum.net.au/learn/animals/mammals/australian-fur-seal/

57 Yancy, P. (1990). *Where is God when it hurts?* Grand Rapids, Michigan: Zondervan.

58 National Ocean Service. (n.d.). *Do volcanoes occur in the ocean?* https://oceanservice.noaa.gov/facts/volcanoes.html

59 United States Geological Survey Science for a Changing World: Volcano Hazard Program. (2018, 29 November). *About volcanos*. https://volcanoes.usgs.gov/vhp/about_volcanoes.html

60 United States Geological Survey Science for a Changing World: Volcano Hazard Program. (n.d.). *Successful crisis response by Indonesia's first-class volcano response team*. Retrieved from https://volcanoes.usgs.gov/vdap/merapi.html

61 United States Geological Survey Science for a Changing World (2014, 23 September). *Indian Ocean Tsunami remembered: Scientists reflect on the 2004 Indian Ocean that killed thousands* https://www.usgs.gov/news/indian-ocean-tsunami-remembered-scientists-reflect-2004-indian-ocean-killed-thousands

62 Dirckx, S. (n.d.). *Where is God to be found in natural disasters?* Zacharias Trust. https://www.zachariastrust.org/why-natural-disasters

63 United States Geological Survey Science for a Changing World: Natural Haz-

ards. (n.d.). *How much of the Earth is volcanic?* https://www.usgs.gov/faqs/how-much-earth-volcanic?qt-news_science_products=0#qt-news_science_products

64 Billy Graham Evangelistic Association. (2020, 10 March). Where Is God in natural disasters? https://billygraham.org/story/where-is-god-in-natural-disasters-2/

65 University of Wisconsin – Madison. (2007, 15 November). What determines sky's colours at sunrise and sunset? https://www.sciencedaily.com/releases/2007/11/071108135522.htm

66 National Geographic. (2019, 15 May). *Rainforests explained.* https://www.nationalgeographic.com/environment/habitats/rain-forests/

67 Global Education. (n.d.). *Forests: A global perspective.* https://www.globaleducation.edu.au/verve/_resources/Forest-global-perspective_web.pdf

68 Haskell, D. G. (2013). The forest unseen: A year's watch in nature. Penguin.

69 *The meaning of Shalom in the Bible.* (n.d.). NIV International Version. https://www.thenivbible.com/blog/meaning-shalom-bible

70 Department of Agriculture, Water and the Environment, Australian Government. (n.d.). *About wetlands.* https://www.environment.gov.au/water/wetlands/about

71 Birdlife Australia. (2014, November). *Migratory* shorebird [factsheet]. http://birdlife.org.au/documents/Shorebirds-Fact Sheet.pdf

72 Interserve. (n.d.). *We are kingdom gardeners.* https://interserve.org.au/kingdomgardeners/

73 Gan, K. (2010). Sermon delivered at BelAir Baptist Church.

74 Mizutani, F., Tanaka, T. & Nakayama, N. (2015). Estimation of optimal metropolitan size in Japan with consideration of social costs. *Empirical Economics, 48*(4): 1713–1730. https://link-springer-com.ezproxy.newcastle.edu.au/article/10.1007/s00181-014-0850-6

75 Wolch, J. R., Byrne, J. & Newell, J. P. (2014). Urban green space, public health, and environmental justice: The challenge of making cities 'just green enough'. *Landscape and Urban Planning, 125*: 234–244. https://doi.org/10.1016/j.landurbplan.2014.01.017

76 Roebuck Bay Working Group Inc. (2017). *Benthos (mud) monitoring.* https://www.roebuckbay.org.au/volunteer-activities/benthos-monitoring/

77 Broome Bird Observatory. (2020). *Witness the spectacular.* http://www.broomebirdobservatory.com/the-migration

78 The Raptor Resource Project. (2017, 19 November). *Eagle eyes.* https://www.raptorresource.org/2017/11/19/eagle-eyes/

79 National Eagle Center. (n.d.). *Eagle eyes.* https://www.nationaleaglecenter.org/eagle-eyes/

80 Palevitz, B. (2001). *Why we say it with flowers.* The Scientist. https://www.the-scientist.com/opinion-old/why-we-say-it-with-flowers-53979

81 Kaplan, S. & Kaplan, R. (1990). *The experience of nature.* Cambridge, England: Cambridge University Press.

82 Holt, A., Vahidinia, S., Gagnon, Y. L., Morse, D. E. & Sweeney, A. M. (2014). Photosymbiotic giant clams are transformers of solar flux. *Journal Royal Society Interface, 11*(101): 20140678. https://doi.org/10.1098/rsif.2014.0678.

83 National Aeronautics and Space Association Earth Observatory. (n.d.). *Mt. Cook, New Zealand.* https://earthobservatory.nasa.gov/images/3578/mt-cook-new-zealand

84 Muir, J. (1894). The Mountains of California. New York: The Century Co.

85 Charles Spurgeon Quotations. (n.d.). Quotetab https://www.quotetab.com/quote/by-charles-spurgeon/purposes-plans-and-achievements-of-men-may-all-disappear-like-yon-cloud-upon-th

86 Martin, C. (2014, 25 June). *'70 million Christians martyred for their faith since Jesus walked the earth.* Christian Today. https://www.christiantoday.com/article/70-million-christians-martyred-faith-since-jesus-walked-earth/38403.htm

87 Ryle, J. C. (2012). Gospel of Luke: Expository thoughts on the gospel. Edinburgh: The Banner of Truth Trust.

88 Fairclough, C. (2013, November). *Currents, waves, and tides: The ocean in motion.* https://ocean.si.edu/planet-ocean/tides-currents/currents-waves-and-tides-ocean-motion

89 Wikipedia. (2020, 20 April). *Wind wave.* https://en.wikipedia.org/wiki/Wind_wave

90 Exploring Our Fluid Earth. (n.d.). *Wave energy and wave changes with depth.* https://manoa.hawaii.edu/exploringourfluidearth/physical/waves/wave-energy-and-wave-changes-depth

91 Lady Elliott Island. (n.d.). *Island history.* https://ladyelliot.com.au/island-history/

92 Wirzba, N. (2015). From nature to creation: A Christian vision for understanding and loving our world. Grand Rapids, Michigan: Baker Academic.

93 Durham, E. (2020, April). *Can staying home help us regain a sense of place?* https://www.christianitytoday.com/ct/2020/april-web-only/earth-day-creation-care-staying-home-regain-sense-of-place.html

www.ingramcontent.com/pod-product-compliance
Lightning Source LLC
Chambersburg PA
CBHW041400050426
42334CB00066B/98